The 20th Century's
Most Influential
HISPANICS

Carlos Santana

Legendary Guitarist

by Adam Woog

LUCENT BOOKS

An imprint of Thomson Gale, a part of The Thomson Corporation

THOMSON
™
GALE

Detroit • New York • San Francisco • New Haven, Conn. • Waterville, Maine • London

For Robert Liddington

For more information, contact
Lucent Books
27500 Drake Rd.
Farmington Hills, MI 48331-3535
Or you can visit our Internet site at http://www.gale.com

LIBRARY OF CONGRESS CATALOGING-IN-PUBLICATION DATA

Woog, Adam, 1953–
   Carlos Santana : legendary guitarist / by Adam Woog.
      p. cm. — (Twentieth century's most influential hispanics)
   Includes bibliographical references and index.
   ISBN-13: 978-1-59018-972-6 (hard cover : alk. paper)
   ISBN-10: 1-59018-972-8 (hard cover : alk. paper)
   1. Santana, Carlos. 2. Rock musicians—United States—Biography. I. Title. II. Series.
ML419.S22W66 2006
787.87'164092—dc22
[B]
                                                          2006010864

Printed in the United States of America

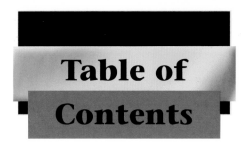

Table of Contents

Foreword

When Alberto Gonzales was a boy living in Texas, he never dreamed he would one day stand next to the president of the United States. Born to poor migrant workers, Gonzales grew up in a two-bedroom house shared by his family of ten. There was no telephone or hot water. Because his parents were too poor to send him to college, Gonzales joined the Air Force, but after two years obtained an appointment to the Air Force Academy and, from there, transferred to Rice University. College was still a time of struggle for Gonzales, who had to sell refreshments in the bleachers during football games to support himself. But he eventually went on to Harvard Law School and rose to prominence in the Texas government. And then one day, decades after rising from his humble beginnings in Texas, he found himself standing next to President George W. Bush at the White House. The president had nominated him to be the nation's first Hispanic attorney general. As he accepted the nomination, Gonzales embraced the president and said, "'Just give me a chance to prove myself'—that is a common prayer for those in my community. Mr. President, thank you for that chance."

Like Gonzales, many Hispanics in America and elsewhere have shed humble beginnings to soar to impressive and previously unreachable heights. In the twenty-first century, influential Hispanic figures can be found worldwide and in all fields of endeavor including science, politics, education, the arts, sports, religion, and literature. Some accomplishments, like those of musician Carlos Santana or author Alisa Valdes-Rodriguez, have added a much-needed Hispanic voice to the artistic landscape. Others, such as revolutionary Che Guevara or labor leader Dolores Huerta, have spawned international social movements that have enriched the rights of all peoples.

But who exactly is Hispanic? When studying influential Hispanics, it is important to understand what the term actually means. Unlike strictly racial categories like "black" or "Asian," the term "Hispanic" joins a huge swath of people from different countries, religions, and races. The category was first used by the U.S. census bureau in 1980 and is used to refer to Spanish-speaking people of any race. Officially, it denotes a person whose ancestry either descends in whole or in part from the people of Spain or from the various peoples of Spanish-speaking Latin America. Often the term "Hispanic" is used synonymously with the term "Latino," but the two actually have slightly different meanings. "Latino" refers to people only from the countries of Latin America, such as Argentina, Brazil, and Venezuela, whether they speak Spanish or Portuguese. Meanwhile, Hispanic refers to only Spanish-speaking peoples but from any Spanish-speaking country, such as Spain, Puerto Rico, or Mexico.

In America, Hispanics are reaching new heights of cultural influence, buying power, and political clout. More than 35 million people identified themselves as Hispanic on the 2000 U.S. census, and there were estimated to be more than 41 million Hispanics in America as of 2006. In the twenty-first century people of Hispanic origin have officially become the nation's largest ethnic minority, outnumbering both blacks and Asians. Hispanics constitute about 13 percent of the nation's total population, and by 2050 their numbers are expected to rise to 102.6 million, at which point they would account for 24 percent of the total population. With growing numbers and expanding influence, Hispanic leaders, artists, politicians, and scientists in America and in other countries are commanding attention like never before.

These unique and fascinating stories are the subjects of *The Twentieth Century's Most Influential Hispanics* collection from Lucent Books. Each volume in the series critically examines the challenges, accomplishments, and legacy of influential Hispanic figures; many of whom, like Alberto Gonzales, sprang from modest beginnings to achieve groundbreaking goals. *The Twentieth Century's Most Influential Hispanics* offers vivid narrative, fully documented primary and secondary source quotes, a bibliography, thorough index, and mix of color and black and white photographs which enhance each volume and provide excellent starting points for research and discussion.

The Guitarist

Throughout a career spanning four decades and still going strong, Carlos Santana has been a major force in popular music. The guitarist and his band—also called Santana—virtually invented Latin rock, a style that merges two passionate genres: the infectious rhythms of Latin music and the driving beat of rock. In so doing, Santana has become one of the world's most prominent Latin musicians and a genuine hero to rock fans—and Latino communities—everywhere.

Santana's most important contribution to music may not be his compositions. Nor is it necessarily his abilities as a bandleader. Santana's significant contribution, in the opinion of many, is twofold. First is his pioneering merger of disparate musical styles; Santana was playing world music (music that has been influenced by folk and pop styles from around the world) before the term was ever coined.

Furthermore, there is his undeniable gift as a guitarist. The fiery, soaring Santana sound is unique; two or three notes are usually enough to identify him. Everything in a Santana solo means something, because the guitarist tries always to find the perfect note for a given moment. Doing so lets him communicate with people directly, he says: "When I hit that note—if I hit it correctly—I hit the umbilical cord of anybody who is listening."[1]

"You Play What Is in Your Soul"

Many forces have shaped Santana's music. The guitarist, having come of age in the fertile rock scene of San Francisco in the late 1960s, is fully at home in that genre. Giants of jazz, particularly trumpeter Miles Davis and saxophonist John Coltrane, have also profoundly influenced him.

Of course, Santana is also steeped in a variety of Latin styles. He was deeply moved by the traditional Mexican music he heard as a

Carlos Santana is known for his virtuoso guitar playing and melding of diverse musical styles.

Music fans cavort in the mud at a 1968 Washington rock festival that featured many bands, including Santana's band.

youth and the emotional solos his violinist father played. He later also absorbed sophisticated Latin-based styles like salsa.

And yet the guitarist is not limited to playing only within these genres. He has experimented with many other forms, acknowledging in particular the deep debt his music owes to African and Caribbean rhythms. Santana refuses to be neatly pigeonholed, commenting: "We are not Xerox machines, we should break down stereotypes. Why should I be limited to just playing Mexican music? . . . If you are alive and have a heart, you play what is in your soul."[2]

Up and Down

Santana's career has had its ups and downs. As a teenaged musicians, he worked hard just to make a living. Fame arrived suddenly, before his band even had a record out.

With celebrity, however, came problems that tore the guitarist's original band apart, and in the years since then his fortunes have periodically dipped and risen. He has sold millions of albums, has been a consistently successful live act, and has picked up multiple Grammy Awards. But at times he has seemed out of step with the rest of the musical world, has released his share of mediocre albums, and has endured sales so poor that, at one point, he could not even get a recording contract. By the late 1990s, it seemed possible that the public could forget the guitarist.

Then came his stunning comeback. Santana's album *Supernatural*, released in 1999, was a blockbuster, shrewdly combining the guitarist's classic sound with the voices and songs of a new generation. The mixture was explosively successful; *Supernatural* sold in the tens of millions. It introduced Santana to a new generation of fans and reminded his old fans that the guitarist was still a powerful force.

Santana rehearses with his band in preparation for a performance at the 2004 Latin Grammy Awards.

Carlos Santana and his wife, Deborah King Santana, arrive at the Academy Awards in February 2005.

Throughout his career, Santana has tried hard to stay humble and declines to think of himself as anything but a person who happens to play the guitar:

> If the people like [my music], great. I equate myself with some great waiter: My napkin is tucked, my apron is clean, the water is pure, and the flowers are fresh. And what [I'm] serving is always tasty. . . . I hope you're hungry. If you're not, no problem. I'm

going to commit suicide because people don't like me? I have seen a lot of musicians go through that, and it's really pathetic.[3]

Spiritual Guidance

In avoiding a life of excess, Santana chose to follow instead a path of meditative spirituality. This interest in spirituality has helped him maintain a healthy sense of himself as a human being, rather than as a music machine or an ego-filled superstar. It has also allowed him to remain gentle and easygoing. His friend and fellow guitarist Eric Clapton remarks simply, "Carlos Santana is the sweetest man I know."[4]

One crucial source of strength has been Santana's family: his three children and his wife, Deborah King Santana. Carlos freely acknowledges that Deborah has helped him through the darkest periods in his life. This has included offering tough love—demanding, in the words of one of his most famous songs, that he change his evil ways. Carlos comments: "Spiritually, emotionally, financially, she's a guiding light. I'd probably be a hobo if it wasn't for her."[5]

Carlos Santana's dedication to spirituality has profoundly shaped not only his personal life but his attitude toward music as well. He often speaks of music's ability to bring together people of different ages, races, and religions: "I'm more clear now as to why I play. It's not just to make people happy or to make them dance—it's to change things: change myself, change the people in my band, change people all over the world, so we can have a clearer vision about life and about ourselves, so we can bring more harmony to the world."[6]

The guitarist's remarkable musical and personal journey has taken him around the world many times—and, through his albums, into the hearts and homes of millions. It began, however, in a humble environment—the small town in Mexico where he was born.

Chapter 1

From Jalisco to San Francisco

arlos Santana's hometown is Autlán de Navarro, a small village in the Mexican state of Jalisco, southeast of Puerto Vallarta and southwest of Guadalajara. When Carlos was young, Autlán had no electricity or running water. The guitarist recalls that when he visited in 1983, it was still rustic: "The village is still the same, there's no fences, no paved roads, no electric lights. There's a few places where they have electricity, but it's still a place in another century."[7]

Carlos Augusto Alves Santana, as he was christened, was born on July 20, 1947. He was the middle child of seven. Antonio, Laura, and Irma were older; Leticia, Jorge, and Maria were younger.

Their parents, José Santana and Josefina Barragan Santana, were strong forces in their children's lives. Carlos comments: "From my mother, I learned that everything in life is borrowed from the Lord. From my father, I learned that life is service. From both parents, I learned good manners."[8]

The Santanas were not wealthy, even by the standards of Autlán, and they moved often as their fortunes rose and fell. Carlos remembers one home in particular: "It was a brick house but it was pretty primitive still. It had a lot of rooms, but I didn't have my own room. Since there were seven of us I always had to share."[9]

Early Musical Memories

Carlos has many other vivid recollections of his early years. But his strongest memories are about music. Sometimes Carlos heard local ensembles play; sometimes it was a traveling group. They had a powerful impact on him:

> It was like when, you know, Cupid throws an arrow and hits you. First, there was this Mexican band, dressed up with bows and arrows. They were playing some funky weird music—I didn't know it yet, but it was like [reggae pioneer] Lee Perry, [funk musician] George Clinton, and [avant-garde jazz man] Sun Ra mixed up; Mexican funky. The second [experience] was Los Indios Tabajara, playing more traditional folk music—songs like "Maria Elena." I remember it piercing me.[10]

These groups certainly had an impact on Carlos's musical development. His most significant early influence, however, was his

Santana grew up listening to the sounds of traditional Mexican mariachi *bands like the one pictured here.*

father, a professional violinist. (Music clearly ran in the family. Carlos's great-grandfather and grandfather were also musicians.)

José Santana, Carlos's father, led a band called Los Cardinales that specialized in *son,* the traditional popular songs of Mexico. He also frequently found work in various *mariachi* bands. *Mariachi* is a type of Mexican dance music, influenced by both Spanish and native music and performed by small orchestras including violins and trumpets.

Beginning the Violin

Son and *mariachi* are dramatic styles. Like all musicians who play them, José had a powerfully emotional playing style. He injected passion into every note he played, making each one count by creating drawn-out, tension-filled melodic lines.

The effect of José's passionate music on people was not lost on his son. Carlos respected his father's charismatic ability to affect people this way. He recalls: "With the violin, I saw how people adored him, literally. Old people, young people, of course women. And I said, That's what I want to do, and what I want to be."[11]

José Santana began teaching the basics of music to his son when Carlos was five, giving him a thorough grounding in music theory and starting him on his first instrument, the violin. Their shared love of music may have been one reason why Carlos felt he was a particular favorite of his father: "All of my sisters and brothers were special but, for some reason, I felt I was the apple of his eye. I felt like I could get away with more. I don't know if it was because I was lighter in skin or he knew I was going to be a musician. All I know was that he was less tolerant with everyone else."[12]

To Tijuana

José was a popular musician, frequently hired for weddings, baptisms, and other celebrations. But work often took him far from home, since opportunities were limited in Autlán. Carlos remembers missing his father terribly when he was gone on these trips. The boy would console himself by imagining hugging José and remembering the way he smelled: a combination of flesh, cologne, and sweat.

In 1954, hoping for steadier work, José moved north to Tijuana, near the U.S. border on Mexico's west coast. Only about 20 miles (32.2 km) from San Diego, Tijuana was (and still is) a popular destination city for American tourists. Because of this, Tijuana—like other border towns—was home to many strip bars, drugs, prostitution, and other seaminess.

After about a year, José's strong-willed wife, Josefina, decided she had had enough of his absence. Carlos recalls, "He was sending money, but we hadn't seen him for a while."[13] Among Josefina's concerns was the worry that her charming husband was involved with other women. Instead of demanding José's return south, Josefina packed up all seven kids and took them north.

American tourists pose for souvenir photos in Tijuana, Mexico. The Santana family moved to this border town in the mid-1950s.

"Like the 'Stars Wars' Cantina"

Josefina's suspicions were confirmed when the family arrived in Tijuana. José was living with another woman. Carlos remembers a loud confrontation on the street outside the house that José was sharing with his new friend.

Once the fight cooled down, José installed his family in a run-down hotel. "He put us in the Colonial Hotel, a really funky place," Carlos recalls. "They were still putting the roof on."[14] At first, José stopped by only occasionally to visit. After a few months, however, he and Josefina made up, and the entire Santana family moved into a house together.

By this time, the kids were attending Catholic school. Carlos hated it, especially the restrictive rules. He much preferred running in the wide-open streets of Tijuana. During this period, Carlos began picking up English, which he learned in part by watching other people's televisions through their fences.

Tijuana was a new world for young Carlos, full of excitement, fun, and a little danger. The boy was a sponge, soaking up everything he could about pop culture and street life. He recalls: "The smell of tacos, the colors, the tourists, [TV cowboy star] Roy Rogers, [boxer] Sugar Ray Robinson, [musicians] Bo Diddley [and] Little Richard—all of that was Tijuana for me. Everything is still very clear in my mind. Tijuana [was] like the 'Star Wars' cantina."[15]

A Big Angel

Even as a child, Santana's spirit seemed special to those around him. His aunt used to say that Carlos had a big angel, meaning that his life was charmed and that someone especially powerful was watching over him. She predicted that he would one day be a bishop in the Catholic Church and preach to thousands.

Quoted in Steve Heilig, "Carlos Santana: An Interview with Steve Heilig," *Whole Earth*, Summer 2000. www.wholeearthmag.com/ArticleBin/375.html.

Thousands of people gather for a 2005 Santana concert performed in Mexico City's main square, El Zocalo.

Earning a Living

But Tijuana also provided a lesson in the sad realities of poverty. Carlos had precious little time for the games and play of childhood. The Santanas were so poor that everyone started work as soon as possible.

One day, José bought a case of chewing gum and divided it in half. He gave the halves to Carlos and his older brother Antonio, telling them grimly not to return until everything was sold. Carlos comments: "In retrospect, I can see why he was so stern about it. He needed help [with expenses]. It was a cold slap in the face for me, but a good lesson. Because, ever since, I'm not afraid of the streets, not at all."[16]

Carlos augmented the family's income in other ways as well. Before reaching his teens, he was busking—playing music for money on the street. With his violin, he joined two guitarists; they dressed up in cowboy outfits to attract tourists and played requests for fifty cents a song—mostly corny tunes like "Cielito Lindo" and "La Bamba." Carlos also played occasionally with his father in bars, but he hated how shabby these places were and how difficult life was for the people who frequented them.

Carlos rebelled during this period against traditional music, because it allowed no deviation from accepted melodies and rhythms. He recalls: "I played simple waltzes and really simple changes. After a while I got tired of it because my father wouldn't let me improvise when I wanted. I would memorize a piece as well as I could and when I tried to play some different notes, my father would stop me."[17] Carlos promised himself that, when he was older, he would play only what he wanted, where he wanted.

"Oh, Man, This Is the Stuff"

In 1960, in search of still better opportunities, José left again. This time, he successfully applied for a U.S. work permit and headed north to San Francisco's sizable Mexican community.

As soon as his father was gone, Carlos quit the violin. He loved music, but he had learned the instrument only to please José. Carlos never got a satisfactory sound from the instrument; he joked that he sounded like Jack Benny, a comedian famous for playing enthusiastically but terribly. Santana disliked the violin so much, he says, that "I hated the way it smelled, the way it sounded and the way it looked—three strikes."[18]

He was drawn instead to the pop music on American radio stations. He was especially taken with electric, urban blues, and the African American dance style called rhythm and blues (R&B)—the genre that would soon evolve into soul music. Carlos's father dismissed these styles as pachuco music—*pachuco* was a derogatory term for a hoodlum—but Carlos was hooked.

He was powerfully attracted to the music's energy. He could also relate to the subject matter—living, loving, drinking, and surviving in a harsh world. And he loved the music's sound. He recalls: "Blues was my first love. It was the first thing where I

During his teen years, Santana became attracted to R&B, a musical genre popularized by groups such as the Drifters (pictured).

said, 'Oh man, this is the stuff.' It just sounded so raw and honest, gutbucket honest."[19]

His First Guitar

Carlos started hanging out wherever blues and R&B musicians performed, sneaking in if necessary. One band in particular caught his attention: the TJs, which specialized in current pop hits like "Green Onions" by Booker T. and the MG's. The TJs' lead guitarist, Xavier Batiz, was a standout with his flashy performance style, flamboyant clothes, and pompadoured hair. Carlos recalls that Batiz "dressed like Little Richard, played like B.B. King, with a little Ray Charles in there. He had a beautiful tone on guitar."[20]

Carlos's father, still in San Francisco, was responsible for giving the boy his first guitar, when Carlos turned twelve. Informed by

Josefina's letters about Carlos's interest in pop music, José sent a beat-up L5 Gibson, a popular style of electric guitar both then and now. Carlos immediately started learning it. The basics came easily, thanks to his early violin and theory training; soon, he had mastered tunes like "Apache," a song by the Shadows that was typical of the guitar-driven instrumentals popular at the time.

His First Job

Carlos was soon good enough to land his first job with a band, the Strangers. This turned out to be short-lived, however. Within four months, he quit to join the house band at a Tijuana club called the Convoy.

Santana began learning to play guitar at the age of 12. Here, he is pictured performing in concert in 1987.

Learning Focus and Determination

Santana's modest upbringing instilled a strong work ethic in him. In this excerpt from a 2000 interview, he comments:

What I want to do with music is pinch people, to see that we all have a passport to some kind of success with our grace and energy. I see a lot of people who come to the USA and don't really want to work; they just stand around. I came here and my mom said, "OK, you're gonna wash dishes, and get a job, you're gonna help with the rent." I learned about responsibility, about two things many people lack—focus and determination.

Quoted in Steve Heilig, "Carlos Santana: An Interview with Steve Heilig," *Whole Earth*, Summer 2000. www.wholeearthmag.com/ArticleBin/375.html.

This group alternated hourly with strip acts, playing from 4:00 P.M. to midnight on weekdays and until 6:00 A.M. on the weekends. When the band was on, it ground out current hits. When off, Carlos and the other band members hung out with strippers and others employed by the club. It was a tough life and a grueling schedule, but it earned Carlos nine dollars a week, which went a long way toward keeping the Santana family solvent.

Furthermore, Carlos was able to hone his guitar chops (skills) every night with invaluable on-the-job training. Sometimes he could even study the techniques of real, live American jazz and R&B musicians. This happened when musicians found themselves stranded in Tijuana and had to scrape together the fare home by playing in clubs like the Convoy.

Meanwhile, on Sundays Carlos offset the worldly, fast-paced life he led during the rest of the week by playing violin in his church orchestra. Carlos was a tough, streetwise teenager, but he was also a proper churchgoing boy. He comments, "So, my life was pretty balanced."[21]

San Francisco

Carlos might have been content to stay in this life indefinitely, but in 1962 (when Carlos was fifteen) the family moved again, joining José in San Francisco. As before, Josefina wanted to keep an eye on her husband. She also felt that the whole family would have a better life in the United States.

Carlos rebelled. He was having too much fun, he felt like an adult already, and he hated the idea of becoming a typical American kid. He recalls: "The stuff they [American teenagers] were talking about was silly. I'm hanging around a bunch of old guys talking about Ray Charles and the blues, and [American kids are] talking about playing hooky and stealing cars and doing some pimply Beach Boy stuff that didn't make any sense to me."[22]

African Roots

When I go to Africa, I am not just some musical tourist—I am part of the family. My values are consistent with the American Indians, aborigines, and African people. . . . I try to honor their music, take certain elements, give it back in a new way, and credit them immediately—financially, emotionally, spiritually—give it right back. There's a way to make [such an exchange] a win-win situation—that's the way of the future.

Quoted in Steve Heilig, "Carlos Santana: An Interview with Steve Heilig," *Whole Earth,* Summer 2000. www.wholeearthmag.com/ArticleBin/375.html.

Eventually, however, the family prevailed, and he agreed to go with them. The Santanas settled in a modest place in San Francisco's Mission District, with the seven kids sharing two bedrooms. Carlos enrolled at nearby James Lick Junior High (now James Lick Middle School). Soon after the move, he also became a U.S. citizen.

But, as he had predicted, Carlos hated San Francisco. He was homesick for Tijuana and hampered by his limited English. He attended school only sporadically and because of this, did poorly. Furthermore, he clashed often with his strong-willed mother. After

Crowds throng the Mexican border. Carlos spent a year on his own in Tijuana in the early 1960s.

one argument too many, Josefina finally gave up, handed him twenty dollars, and said he could go back to Mexico.

To Tijuana and Back Again

Arriving in Tijuana, Carlos was alone and a little scared. His first stop was to one of the city's main houses of worship, the Church of the Virgin of Guadalupe, to pray for a job. He next went to the Convoy Club, where he immediately got his old gig back— his replacement had just quit.

Carlos stayed in Tijuana for almost a year on his own. But his family missed him, and his mother regretted having sent him away. In the late fall of 1963, his parents and older brother traveled south to convince Carlos to return to San Francisco, and he reluctantly agreed. José recalls his son's sullenness on the long drive back: "He was mad. He did not say a single word during the whole trip."[23]

Once again, Carlos enrolled in school and got together with bass player Dan Haro and drummer Gus Rodriguez. Their band played occasionally at gigs like parties and weddings. Once, backing a female R&B singer, the band even made it to the finals in a radio station contest at the Cow Palace, a well-known auditorium. They didn't win, but just getting to the finals boosted the guitarist's confidence.

Hesitant to Emigrate

When my family was ready to emigrate, Carlos did not want to come. He said he liked Mexico too much to leave it. We postponed our trip a few days as we tried to persuade our son to come with us. Then, all of a sudden, he hid from us.

José Santana, quoted in Marc Shapiro, *Carlos Santana: Back on Top*. New York: St. Martin's, 2000, p.23.

In 1963, Carlos moved on to Mission High School. He also found an after-school job, washing dishes and flipping burgers with his brother Antonio at the Tic Tock Diner. Santana recalls: "That's how I bought my first amplifier. We kept the kitchen clean and cooked French fries and burgers. I hated the smell of the bleach we used to mop the floor. I'll never forget it."[24]

Influences

In his free hours, he spent all of his energy on music. Carlos was still listening intently to blues and R&B. Most of the musicians in these styles whom he admired were from an older generation. But Carlos was also listening to players closer to his own age.

He was particularly interested in musicians who were merging blues with the newer, louder, rougher sounds of rock. Three guitarists especially moved him: Jimi Hendrix, Eric Clapton (then playing with Cream), and Mike Bloomfield of the Paul Butterfield Blues Band.

Carlos was also drawn to the more abstract, sophisticated world of jazz. He was fascinated by, among others, the experiments of tenor saxophonist John Coltrane and trumpeter Miles Davis. He was also intrigued by an unusual combination of guitar and Latin percussion created by bandleader Chico Hamilton and his guitarist, Hungarian-born Gabor Szabo.

Furthermore, Carlos was right in the middle of one of the most important developments in rock music: the San Francisco psychedelic scene. Psychedelic rock was short-lived but extremely influential. It was integral to the burgeoning hippie movement and everything this entailed, from drugs and anti-war protests to free love, underground newspapers, and outdoor "be-ins" that featured wild music and dancing.

Janis Joplin performs with her band Big Brother and the Holding Company in Monterey, California, in 1967. Joplin was part of the psychedelic rock music scene which influenced Santana and countless other musicians.

Psychedelic music was emerging all over the country, but the volatile and exciting San Francisco scene was its undisputed center. From the dozens of bands in the area, several were emerging on top, among them Jefferson Airplane, Big Brother and the Holding Company, and the Grateful Dead. Carlos loved them all.

Life After High School

Despite his disinclination to attend school, Carlos graduated from Mission High in 1965. But the tension between him and his mother had never resolved itself. He recalls: "Mom wanted me to live according to her rigid sense of right and wrong. I was a hippie, and we couldn't talk about anything, so I moved out."[25]

It was time for Carlos to strike out on his own. Soon after graduation, he moved out of the family home and into the first in a series of small, run-down apartments shared with other aspiring musicians. Everyone was broke all the time, he recalls: "We were always hungry."[26]

In addition to working at the Tic Tock, Carlos occasionally played gigs with his father or with his unnamed band, and he continued to busk on the street periodically. But he was not yet a professional musician, someone who made a living at it. That would come—spectacularly—in the next phase of his career.

Chapter 2

The Santana Blues Band

In 1966, Carlos Santana, dishwasher and aspiring guitarist, made his stage debut at an important venue: the Fillmore Auditorium in San Francisco. This was not just an exciting moment in the young musician's career; it was a pivotal, life-changing event. Santana would never be the same again.

The run-down but lively Fillmore was the most important gathering spot for rock lovers in the San Francisco Bay Area. All of the top national bands played there, and performing there was a breakout moment for any local band.

Santana hung out at the Fillmore whenever he could. Sometimes he paid to get in, but other times he sneaked in. This required dodging Bill Graham, the hall's tough-talking, larger-than-life owner and operator. Graham was the city's most powerful concert promoter, famous for pairing dissimilar groups on the same bill. During the Fillmore's glory days, fans could hear top jazz, blues, and hard rock bands all in the same evening. It was an amazing, eclectic education, Santana recalls:

> My university was . . . the Fillmore. That's the place
> that I hung out. . . . Bill Graham used to scream at me

Cream perform at the Fillmore Auditorium in San Francisco.

and throw me out because I didn't have any money, but I'd sneak in. I had to see the Grateful Dead, I had to see Cream, I had to see [jazzmen] Buddy Rich and Charles Lloyd and Roland Kirk, Miles [Davis], and I didn't care if he screamed at me. After a while, he just put up with me.[27]

First Appearance at the Fillmore

When Santana made his first appearance at the Fillmore in 1966, he found himself onstage almost by accident. Paul Butterfield, a renowned Chicago blues harmonica player and the leader of the scheduled band, could not perform. In his absence, a loose jam session was hastily organized, and the performers (including Mike Bloomfield and Al Kooper, the organist for Blood, Sweat, and Tears) agreed to let Santana sit in.

Both Graham and Bloomfield were favorably impressed with Santana's fiery playing. A local guitarist named Tom Frazier also heard Santana play that evening. Frazier invited him to a jam session in nearby Mountain View. This was the first meeting between Santana and organist-singer Gregg Rolie, who would soon become a key part of the Santana band.

Forming a Band

Santana, Frazier, and Rolie got along well and later in 1966 decided to form a band. Other players came and went, and Frazier soon left. Santana and Rolie emerged as the group's core and main musical forces.

Despite this turnover, one thing remained steady: In addition to a drummer who played a standard trap set, the band always had a second percussionist. This musician played a type of hand-struck drums, of Afro-Caribbean origin, called conga drums. The addition of congas was unusual at the time, and it set the band apart from others. Santana recalls: "We started mixing up jazz and blues, and some African flavor. We had something different than what was being played [elsewhere]. John Mayall, Eric Clapton, all those guys, were all playing blues—just louder [than earlier blues musicians]. We mixed [the blues] up with the African, the Cuban."[28]

The musicians agreed that their fledgling group would have no formal leader. In theory, each member had an equal vote about musical direction, business affairs, and other matters. Nonetheless, the group decided to name itself after its guitarist. It became the Santana Blues Band.

According to some sources, this decision was made because of a Musicians' Union requirement that bands name a single person as leader. According to the guitarist himself, however, the group chose the name simply because it sounded good: "Santana was something that could be a galaxy. It could be a planet or it could be the winds. It had a universal resonance to it."[29]

Developing a Style

By 1967, the band's lineup was fairly steady. In addition to Santana and Rolie, it included bassist David Brown and drummer Bob

"Doc" Livingston. Marcus Malone and Mike Carabello alternated in the conga-drum position.

The group continued to work out a sound that combined high-energy rock with blues and added percussion. Santana's playing, in particular, was developing, with characteristics not heard elsewhere among rock guitarists. His distinctive style was coming into its own, using elements like drawn-out methods of phrase-building inspired by his father's storytelling and violin playing. "He knew how to create tension," Santana says of his father. "[That's] where I learned to build a guitar solo. Got to tell a story, man."[30]

Other elements of a distinctive style were phrasings and rhythms inspired by Santana's childhood memories, using his guitar to create voicelike solos. For example, he notes, some rhythmic phrases originated with the sound of his mother scolding him: "'Didn't-I-tell-you-not-to-duh-duh-duh-duh. And-I'm-going-to-spank-you!' You can cuss or you can pray with the guitar."[31]

Bill Graham (right), pictured with Paul Kantner and Grace Slick of Jefferson Airplane, gave Santana his opportunity to play onstage at Graham's Fillmore Auditorium.

A Pioneer

Santana formed his signature sound early on, when he was still a teenaged blues guitarist just forming his first real band. In this passage, a younger Latino guitarist, Henry Garza of Los Lonely Boys, comments:

He's a pioneer of Latin rock & roll: His music was something new, but it was intertwined with everything else that was out there at the time—Sixties rock, Latin jazz and more. We're trying to do the same thing with Los Lonely Boys—make a lot of different types of music into something our own—but he did that first. He incorporated his culture into the music, and he mixed English and Spanish in the lyrics. . . .

You could hear his ethnicity in his music—even when he's playing like some blues cat, he still sounds like Santana. And his music always has that rhythm. . . . His playing is both simple and complicated—he can communicate with just one or two notes. He speaks languages through his music that people can understand in any country, any language.

Henry Garza, "Carlos Santana," *Rolling Stone*, April 21, 2005, p. 98.

In the Hospital

The Santana Blues Band's mix of styles was a bracing change of pace from most bands in those heady days of psychedelia. The band was tougher and earthier than other San Francisco bands. Despite their distinctive sound, the band was not getting much recognition. Santana was still working at the Tic Tock and the others still had day jobs as well.

But the group was also slowly beginning to attract some attention, at gigs in clubs like the Ark and the Matrix. One important early appearance was at a free-form hippie gathering, the Human Be-In, in San Francisco's Golden Gate Park early in 1967. The thousands of people who heard the band that day— estimates of the crowd range from ten thousand to thirty thousand —comprised, by far, its largest audience to date.

Musicians perform at the Human Be-In, held in San Francisco's Golden Gate Park in 1967. The Santana Blues Band also played at the event, which attracted thousands.

During this period, Santana fell ill with tuberculosis, a highly contagious and sometimes deadly respiratory disease. The guitarist spent several months in San Francisco General Hospital, confined to an isolation ward with other tuberculosis patients. Life on the ward was dull; there was nothing to keep him occupied, Santana remembers, "but do pottery and watch TV and just watch people die."[32] When the boredom finally became too much to handle, Santana simply left. His doctors were worried that he might still be contagious, but the guitarist convinced them that it would be fine.

Playing the Fillmore

Santana's hospitalization had several consequences. One was that, because of the lingering effects of his illness, he was deferred from the draft for the Vietnam War, then at its height. Another was that during his absence the band nearly fell apart. The others had grown disorganized, and practice sessions were sporadic. Drug and alcohol abuse—already a problem with several members—played a role in this lack of focus.

Santana was not entirely immune to the allure of drugs himself. Though he was never a serious drinker, the guitarist was fond of marijuana and the occasional psychedelic drug such as LSD. However, he never let drugs become more important than the music, and once he was out of the hospital he focused on maintaining the band.

This renewed drive led to another important gig in June 1967: the group's debut at the Fillmore Auditorium. On this occasion the band opened for Paul Butterfield—one of Santana's longtime idols, and probably the man indirectly responsible for the guitarist's first appearance at the Fillmore. The Santana Blues Band was still so obscure that its name was left off posters advertising the event.

"I'm Going to Do That"

Despite this oversight, it was a thrilling moment for the young guitarist. (Still a teenager, he would turn twenty the following month.) Santana's excitement over the Fillmore gig was so great that he even reconciled with his parents over it. He had been estranged from his family for some time, primarily because his mother disapproved so strongly of his lifestyle. Now, however, Santana got back in touch; his father recalls: "He finally called us one day. He said, 'Mama, they're going to let me play at this place on Market Street called the Fillmore.'"[33]

A band plays at San Francisco's Fillmore Auditorium, where the Santana Blues Band made its debut in June 1967.

A poster advertises a series of Santana band concerts. After the group's success at the Fillmore Auditorium, Carlos Santana took a chance on a full-time career as a musician.

The band was well received at the Fillmore, and Santana was buoyed by this and other successes. He finally decided to quit his day job and take a chance on playing music full-time. The day he quit was the day he saw a group of famous San Francisco rockers roll up to the Tic Tock. "The Grateful Dead pulled over in limousines to get some hamburgers," he recalls. "And I'm in my apron, washing dishes and busing tables, and I said, 'I'm going to do that.' Something in me just said, 'If they can do this, I can do this!'"[34] The guitarist quit on the spot and never again held a job beyond that of musician.

Bill Graham Steps In

Graham, the Fillmore's owner, now entered the scene in a major way, playing a pivotal role in the Santana band's rising success. He hired the group often, because he liked its cross-cultural sound and appreciated the fact that it was ethnically diverse at a time when that was still unusual. Graham also liked the group's willingness to step in at the last second and replace canceled acts. Santana recalls: "Every time somebody would miss [a gig], we would be there in a second. I mean, we were hanging around anyway. We didn't have no place else to go."[35]

As a result, the band—which during this period shortened its name to Santana—opened for a number of top acts around the Bay Area. Among these were such stars as the Who, Chicago, Johnny Winter, and Steppenwolf. At almost every gig, the band's high-energy performance proved wildly successful. Santana recalls: "We'd open for those bands, and we'd end up taking [winning over] the crowd. That gave us a lot of confidence that what we had was really working."[36]

A Record Contract and a Recording Debut

Graham helped in other ways, including handling concert bookings and other business matters. One of Graham's varied activities was to book groups for a growing phenomenon: outdoor rock festivals, which were popping up across the country. In this capacity, he was able to arrange appearances by the Santana band for many landmark festivals, including the Monterey (California) Pop Festival and the

Sky River Rock Festival in Sultan, Washington. Although it had yet to tour extensively outside the Bay Area, the group thus began to gather a national reputation.

Meanwhile, the San Francisco sound was becoming a hot commodity nationwide. Major record companies were eager to sign up groups from the area, and several labels expressed interest in the Santana band. Santana favored Columbia, and the Columbia executives liked what they heard. In 1968, the band signed a contract with Columbia for a modest advance.

Adding the Latin Sound

Everyone—band members, Graham, and Columbia executives alike—agreed that the group needed to refine itself before recording. It was a promising but raw ensemble, whose free-form, spontaneous jams were unsuited to the constraints of an album. The group had thought little about creating structured, formal songs, Rolie recalls: "At the time, we were just playing. We didn't think about it."[37]

Graham was instrumental in changing the Santana group from this powerful but loose jam band into a tight, professional ensemble. He helped the players understand how to refine their long jams into structured songs. Even more importantly, Graham dramatically changed the group's sound by introducing Santana and the other musicians to the world of Latin percussion.

Specifically, Graham pointed Santana toward a rhythmically complex style of music called salsa. This infectious Afro-Cuban-Puerto Rican music, typified by artists like Tito Puente, was popular among Latino communities in New York and other East Coast cities, and it was influencing many jazz musicians there. However, salsa had not yet become widely popular, and Graham thought the Santana band would cause a sensation by incorporating the genre. He helped the group learn the basics of salsa and add several well-known songs, including "Oye Como Va," to its repertoire.

Making a Poor Record

By early 1969, the group felt ready to start recording. Santana and the other band members traveled to Los Angeles to begin a session with a Columbia Records staff producer, David Rubinson. The band had made great strides, but problems remained. One was that the group had few original songs in its repertoire. The songs it did know were mostly cover versions of pieces written by others, in an era when original songs were increasingly important elements in attracting listeners.

A more serious concern was the uneven quality of the band's musicianship. Personal problems were hurting the percussion section.

Compounding these problems was the constraint the band felt when it entered the recording studio. Rubinson, the producer, wanted to hear crisply concise songs, but the musicians still wanted to stretch out in long, loose jams. Because of these conflicts, the music recorded in Los Angeles was of such poor quality that it was never released.

Because of creative conflicts with Columbia Records producer David Rubinson (pictured), the first songs recorded by the Santana band were never released.

Working in the Studio

The band returned to San Francisco dispirited, but its percussion section and its fortunes were about to change. Mike Carabello, who had played with the band in its earliest days, replaced conga player Marcus Malone. Carabello brought with him a Nicaraguan-born musician, José "Chepito" Areas, a virtuoso Latin percussionist. And a young drummer, Mike Shrieve, replaced Doc Livingston.

The band was now a sextet: Santana, Rolie, Brown, Shrieve, Carabello, and Areas. This group—the "classic" Santana lineup—felt right, and everything fell into place quickly. Music journalist Simon Leng writes, "The addition of Chepito Areas, coupled with the excellent, sensitive drumming of Michael Shrieve, provided the missing elements in the Santana jigsaw."[38]

The band started work on a new set of studio recordings with a new producer, Brent Dangerfield, and this time the recordings worked. A well-respected blues pianist, Alberto Gianquinto, helped out on some songs, and the sound was stripped down, more intense, and clearly focused. The album was completed, to everyone's satisfaction, in just a week.

A Family Thing

Carlos Santana's music is a family thing for Chicanos [Latinos of Mexican descent]. It's what you listen to when you're all hanging out: Drinking some beers, listening to "Oye Como Va" and cooking some barbecue is the best thing in the world. His music hits right down to the pump—right to the heart. Carlos isn't the lead singer, but he is the maestro.

Los Lonely Boys musician Henry Garza, "Carlos Santana," *Rolling Stone*, April 21, 2005, p. 98.

But the album was not out yet, and the band was still largely unknown outside of the Bay Area. Graham, eager for this to change, arranged for the band to play a number of dates across the country. Among these were prestigious gigs like the Atlantic City (New Jersey) Pop Festival and the Texas International Pop Festival in Dallas.

Santana and bassist David Brown (left) play at the 1969 Woodstock Music Festival, an event that thrust Santana to the forefront of the rock music scene.

Woodstock

Far and away the most important of these appearances was at an outdoor gathering held in August 1969 on a farm near Woodstock, New York. No one knew beforehand what the Woodstock Festival would become: half a million people celebrating three days of high-powered music and free-wheeling joy during the so-called Summer of Love. The event was a touchstone event for a generation and a powerful symbol of the 1960s era; for Santana, it was the chance of a lifetime.

The Santana band played Woodstock because Graham was owed a favor. The festival's promoters needed his help in lining up some of the bigger bands they wanted. He agreed on one condition: that the Santana band be added to the schedule in a prime spot on Saturday night.

Santana gave a blistering performance, arguably the biggest turning point in the guitarist's entire career. Before it, he was virtually unknown and did not even have an album out; after it, he hit the very big time.

Chapter 3

The Big Time

Santana's explosive performance at Woodstock and the band's appearances elsewhere that summer fed a growing word-of-mouth buzz about the group. The multiethnic ensemble, its Latin-drenched sound, and the band's amazing guitarist were hot topics among rock fans. An appearance on *The Ed Sullivan Show*, the nation's top TV variety program, helped raise the public's awareness even more.

A Sensuous Sound

What impressed me [about the band] is that it was an attempt at fusing rock and Afro and Latino and getting a rhythmic sensuous sound into rock, which I've always felt it lacked.

Bill Graham, quoted in Marc Shapiro, *Carlos Santana: Back on Top*. New York: St. Martin's, 2000, p. 67.

Typical of the growing number of Santana fans across the country was Patrick MacDonald, the longtime rock critic for the *Seattle Times*. MacDonald remembers being electrified when the unknown band played at an outdoor concert: "It was such a new sound, but so in tune with what was happening then, that the crowd went nuts."[40]

On Record and Film

Meanwhile, the band's record, called simply *Santana*, was being readied. When it was released in October 1969, critics raved about it, and—after an initial disappointment—the public loved it too. The disappointment was the first single, "Jingo," which stalled at number fifty-six on the sales charts; a catchier tune, "Evil Ways," did much better, reaching number nine.

But *Santana's* real strength turned out to be not in singles but in its album sales. This was part of an overall trend in American pop away from short singles and toward lengthier tunes. The 45-rpm single had dominated pop music sales for years, but in the rock era it was giving way to the wider musical horizons that albums offered.

Santana soared up the *Billboard* sales chart (*Billboard* was, and still is, an influential music-industry magazine). The record was also

Santana's electric performance at the Woodstock Music Festival galvanized the estimated half a million people in attendance.

heavily featured on rock radio across the country. Its longer songs perfectly suited the format of then-popular "underground" FM stations, whose disc jockeys—priding themselves on being anticommercial—sometimes played entire album sides without interruption.

The album quickly climbed to number four. It ultimately spent two years on the charts and sold over 2 million copies. Sales were boosted considerably in 1970, when the wildly popular documentary movie *Woodstock* was released. The Santana band's appearance in this film version of the event was a revelation for millions of fans who had never seen it live.

Hearing about the band was one thing, and hearing it on record was another. But seeing it live and in action, with its multicultural members working together, was an amazing and inspiring experience. Leng writes, "After the release of *Woodstock* on film, Santana became a symbol of racial integration and third world achievement."[41]

The Follow-Up Album

Santana and the other members of the band were, of course, delighted with the album's critical and commercial success. Hoping to keep the momentum going, they quickly began work on a follow-up. The result was *Abraxas*.

An Instant Connection

In its early days, the percussion of the Santana Blues Band was focused on African rhythms. Santana and the other members of his band did not begin consciously incorporating salsa and other forms of Latin music into their sound until introduced to them by manager Bill Graham. Santana notes that this direction toward Latin music proved to be a good one for the band when they began playing gigs on the East Coast, where salsa was already popular. He recalls: "We started doing those songs, and people would sing along. It was an instant connection with the audience."

Quoted in Steve Heilig, "Carlos Santana: An Interview with Steve Heilig," *Whole Earth*, Summer 2000. www. wholeearthmag.com/ArticleBin/375.html.

This second album, released in 1970, was considerably more sophisticated, musically speaking, than *Santana*. It had a subtler, spacier sound, and it used more advanced studio techniques. For example, the songs blended seamlessly from one to the next, a technique prominently used on recent albums by the Beatles and other bands. Carried over from the first album, of course, were what made the band special: its emphasis on percussion and Carlos Santana's expressive guitar solos.

Abraxas's innovative sound was even more popular than the group's debut. The album quickly hit the coveted number one spot, remained there for a year and a half, and ultimately sold more than 4 million copies. In addition, it generated two hit singles, both cover versions: "Black Magic Woman," originally recorded by Fleetwood Mac (which, at the time, was a blues-rock unit) and "Oye Como Va," by salsa king Tito Puente.

Abraxas proved to be the commercial and artistic peak of Carlos Santana's early career. Many fans and critics consider it the best album the guitarist ever made—and, indeed, one of the best rock albums ever made by anyone. MacDonald, the *Seattle Times* critic, comments that when *Abraxas* came out, "I . . . couldn't keep 'Oye Como Va' out of my head. But the [album's] staying power is due to 'Black Magic Woman,' a signature Santana tune because of its intensity and great guitar solo."[42]

Noisy Crickets

The band's sudden success, onstage and on record, brought them more than critical acclaim. After years of near poverty, Santana and the other musicians were now quite rich. Sudden wealth can change one's life for the better; for instance, Santana was able to buy his parents a duplex building in the Noe Valley neighborhood of San Francisco.

The guitarist also bought himself a new home. People who wanted part of his wealth constantly hounded him. The guitarist recalls: "People were knocking on my door at three in the morning—'Won't you do a benefit for me?' And it just became really hard to exist."[43]

Santana moved to rural Mill Valley. Being away from a city for the first time since his childhood, he discovered, was a difficult adjustment. He recalls, "You're used to hearing people stealing tires, and all you hear is crickets."[44]

Noisy crickets, of course, are not a very serious problem (and many people would not consider them a problem at all). However, other aspects of the lifestyle Santana could now lead were very serious indeed. And some of these aspects were increasingly scary—specifically, the problem of drug abuse.

The Pitfalls of Drugs

For those in the band who were susceptible, more money meant better and more frequent drugs. In particular, David Brown and Mike Carabello were becoming seriously involved with hard drugs, and it was affecting their playing abilities. Santana comments: "You're going from a Mission District kid with nothing to having everything—you're Number One, buy your mom a house. [But there's also] too much drugs, everything to excess."[45]

Santana himself was mostly able to avoid this problem. He had occasionally used marijuana and psychedelics for years and did not condemn them. But he disapproved of harder drugs like cocaine and heroin, in large part because he understood how they could affect one's playing abilities.

This was forcefully demonstrated to Santana when he met one of his idols, the legendary Jimi Hendrix. (Although Hendrix made a memorable appearance at Woodstock, the two guitarists had not met there.) Their first meeting came in New York City shortly after the first Santana album's release, when Hendrix's girlfriend invited Santana to a party at Electric Ladyland, Hendrix's recording studio.

As the two guitarists chatted, Hendrix complimented the younger musician on his playing and on his album's success. Hendrix then began to work in the studio, but he was high—so high, in fact, that he had to be taken home. A few months later, Santana attended a Hendrix show in Berkeley, California. The star was, again, so stoned that he could barely perform. Santana recalls, "I could see by his eyes that, by that point, he was deeply married to [drugs]."[46]

Musical Differences

Escalating drug use was a major cause of growing tension within the Santana band. Those who mostly avoided drugs, like

Legendary guitarist Jimi Hendrix was one of Carlos Santana's musical idols.

Santana, were increasingly pitted against serious users like Brown and Carabello. But there were other causes of tension as well.

The most serious differences were between Rolie and Santana, the group's primary musical forces. Rolie loved the then-current progressive rock movement, whose most prominent exponents were bands like Yes; Genesis; Pink Floyd; and Emerson, Lake, and Palmer. Rolie was eager to adopt this genre's trappings—extended instrumentals influenced by classical music, for instance, and concept albums that delivered serious messages.

A Different Path

Meanwhile, Santana was drawn to two other, very different aspects of music. He wanted to emphasize his Latin heritage by increasing the band's emphasis on percussion and adding more Latin-based songs. He was also increasingly moved by the pioneering jazz-rock experiments of performers like Weather Report and Miles Davis. (Davis had many styles throughout his career, but in the early 1970s he was experimenting fruitfully with a combination of jazz and rock.)

The tension between Santana and Rolie grew stronger, and the bickering became more intense. Santana admits that he was sometimes the cause of the fighting: "I know they [the other band members] think I'm crazy because I used to contradict myself so much. I would demand this, I would say this and the next time I would be . . . worse than them."[47] The guitarist also recalls that he sometimes had to threaten the others to get his way:

> In the past, things had been very democratic. But the band did not want the songs "Oye Como Va" and "Samba Pa Ti" on [Abraxas]. They said it didn't sound like Santana. We went back and forth for a long time before I finally said, "Either those two songs go on the album or you go find another guitar player." I had to dig in my heels and it worked.[48]

Another Guitarist Joins Up

Even after Abraxas was released and became monstrously successful, tensions remained. To the public, the band was on top of the rock

Altamont

The Woodstock Festival made Santana famous, and even an appearance at the infamous Altamont festival at
the end of the Summer of Love, 1969,
could not stop the guitarist's growing
fame. Altamont was a huge, free outdoor
concert at Altamont Speedway near San
Francisco. The Rolling Stones headlined,
and Bay Area favorites the Grateful Dead
and Jefferson Airplane were among the
other bands appearing that day.

It should have been a wonderful time,
but the day turned violent and ugly. A
notorious motorcycle gang, the Hell's
Angels, had been hired to provide securi-
ty, and Santana watched in horror from
the stage as the Angels beat a number of
people severely. The day ended with one
murder, three accidental deaths, numer-
ous assaults, and general disarray. Many
observers felt that the Altamont disaster
was the opposite of Woodstock—a symbolic end to the peaceful and idealistic
hippie movement.

heap—a model of ethnic solidarity and cohesive musicianship. In
truth, it was drifting apart, split by individual concerns, and Santana
was increasingly sad and confused. He comments:

> I would turn on the radio and *Abraxas* would be on
> every station, just about. And I found myself more
> and more depressed, and I'd find myself crying. The
> band was deteriorating, and my friends who I grew up
> with were total strangers to me. We started sounding
> like crap. . . . It was basically too much too soon:
> excess, big egos, myself included.[49]

These egos continued to clash as the band continued to tour
and started to prepare its third album. The problem took a dramatic turn late in 1970, when Rolie and Shrieve heard a fifteen-
year-old guitar prodigy, Neal Schon, play. Blown away by
Schon's talent, they began pressuring the others to add him to
the band. Eric Clapton also wooed Schon for his new band,
Derek and the Dominoes, but ultimately the teen guitarist chose
the Santana band.

"A Radiant . . . Peacock"

Being in a relationship with Carlos was like standing beside a radiant, iridescent peacock with its tail feathers fully fanned out in a blue-green rainbow. Everywhere we went, people wanted to shake his hand, praise him. Women actually asked to kiss him right in front of me.

Deborah Santana, *Space Between the Stars*. New York: Ballantine, 2005, p. 204.

Santana had mixed feelings about having a second guitarist. In some ways he was pleased to have a foil he could play off, someone who could inspire him to new heights. In other ways, however, he felt deeply threatened; Schon shared Rolie's interest in progressive rock, and Santana feared that the band's direction would tilt more that way as the younger guitarist asserted himself within the group.

More Personnel Changes

Despite the band's problems, it remained together and began a series of long tours with Schon. These included sold-out concert dates across Europe, a tour with the legendary jazz trumpeter Miles Davis, and long swings through Asia and Africa.

Just before one of these tours began, in February 1971, a medical emergency caused another change in the band's lineup. Chepito Areas, after missing rehearsals, was found near death in his apartment. He had suffered a brain aneurysm—a dangerous bulging of a blood vessel. He survived, but he faced months of recuperation.

Some of the band members wanted to postpone the tour while Areas was in the hospital, arguing that the percussionist was so integral to the band that without him it could not continue. Santana disagreed; he insisted that they find a replacement and fulfill their tour obligations. The guitarist prevailed, and veteran Willie Bobo was briefly added to the lineup before being replaced, in turn, with another talented veteran, Coke Escovedo.

By the time the band completed the tour and returned to San Francisco, Areas had made a complete recovery. He was immediately brought back into the group, and Escovedo was kept as well. Santana was delighted with the inclusion of both Areas and Escovedo, since the addition of an extra percussionist bolstered the guitarist's push for a stronger Latin influence within the band.

Santana III

In the summer of 1971, the band, now an octet, started making a new album. Its official title was simply *Santana*, but to avoid confusion with the first album it is generally called *Santana III*. Some critics have argued that it was a sign of the band's growing distress that it could not agree on a more distinctive title.

Dull title notwithstanding, and despite the album's uncertain mix of styles reflecting the ongoing musical wars within the band, *Santana III* was another smash. It reached number one on the album charts, sold 2 million copies, and generated two hit singles, "Everybody's Everything" and "No One to Depend On." Critics raved as well. Typical was *Rolling Stone* magazine: "This

Santana performs with jazz singer Leon Thomas in 1972.

is music to dance to, but it is music that shrieks for more advanced, dexterous and imaginative dancing than some of the free-form body motion that rock dancing has accepted."[50]

However, the experience of recording the album, even more stressful than before, exhausted Santana. He found some relief by doing what he loved best—playing before an audience—when the band played several concerts around the Bay Area. Notable among these was a gala that the band headlined on the last night before its old stomping grounds, the Fillmore, closed permanently. The occasion was a massive, celebratory jam session that lasted until five o'clock in the morning.

The Beginning of the End

But even a joyous occasion like an all-night jam could not slacken the tension. In particular, the personal rancor between Santana and his old friend Mike Carabello was near the breaking point. As Carabello's drug use increased, the conga drummer had become more and more distant; he was now frequently skipping rehearsals and keeping company with some very shady people.

Just before the band was due to leave for a tour of the East Coast and South America, Santana decided he could not bear Carabello's presence any longer. The guitarist gave the group an ultimatum. It could continue with himself or with Carabello, but not both.

In a move surprising to many, the majority of the group sided with Carabello. Carlos Santana stayed at home, and the Santana band left San Francisco to perform, for the first time, without its namesake. The plan was that Schon would cover all of the guitar parts.

However, audiences and concert promoters quickly realized that the band's original guitarist—the man many considered the heart of the group—was missing. In the wake of multiple complaints, Carabello agreed to leave the band. This turned into a mass exodus, with manager Stan Marcum, bassist Brown, and percussionist Areas also leaving.

The Breakup

Carlos Santana now faced a problem. With Carabello gone, the guitarist could return to the band—but the group had no bass player and a weakened percussion section. Partial relief came when bassist Doug Rauch (who had substituted for Brown in the past) stepped in. As for the percussion, for the first few shows, a roadie (a band employee who sets up equipment) stood in front of a set of conga drums and pretended to play. Soon, however, an East Coast musician, James "Mingo" Lewis, was hired to complete the tour.

Things were falling apart fast. In Puerto Rico, Rolie and Santana got into a fistfight. Then the South American leg of the tour was cut short when the group's gear was confiscated in Peru after the military dictatorship there called the band an unwanted intruder. Dispirited, the group returned to San Francisco.

The Conductor

Carlos was a speechless conductor. He tiptoed across the stage, dark eyes flashing as he connected with each musician, willing to let them play their hardest, their best.

Deborah Santana, *Space Between the Stars*. New York: Ballantine, 2005, p. 190.

Then, during sessions for a fourth album in December 1971, Rolie and Schon made a dramatic announcement: They were leaving the band to form a new group called Journey. They made it clear to Santana that they would be willing to work with him in the studio in some capacity, but the band was breaking up.

Letting Everyone Grow

Understandably for a group of seasoned musicians and strong-willed individuals, everyone had an opinion about the breakup. According to Rolie, each member bore some of the responsibility, though the brunt was borne by Santana. Rolie states: "Everybody had a hand in why it went by the wayside. But a large part of it was due to Carlos's desire to be the true leader of a band that was very democratic and we didn't choose to follow."[51]

Santana had a different take on the matter. In his opinion, it was simply a question of everyone's need for room to change and evolve: "I think it's what happens in most bands. If you've

After his band split up in the early 1970s, Santana mostly played as a solo artist. Here, he performs in London a few years after the breakup.

played out everything you can play with that particular band, you need to let those people go so you can grow musically and spiritually."[52]

And that was that. Within just a few years, the Santana band had gone from obscurity to superstardom—and then had self-destructed. The guitarist would continue to make music, but from this point on it would be essentially as a solo artist with backing. (He retained the legal right to use the name "Santana" for his various groups. This was logical enough; it was, after all, his own name.)

Another major milestone in Carlos Santana's personal and professional life had passed. The breakup was traumatic, but it opened new doors and sent the guitarist down new paths. Santana was about to enter another phase of his life, one that would find him investigating unknown areas of personal and professional growth.

Chapter 4

Love Devotion Surrender

In the wake of the band's breakup, Santana's personal life seemed overdue for a change of pace. He had been a major celebrity for several years, the creation of the last two albums had been difficult, and the breakup of the band had been as traumatic as a messy divorce. The guitarist needed a change and a way of living that would help him avoid the pitfalls of celebrity.

The need for this was brought home forcefully to Santana by seeing the effects of drug abuse on rock's aristocracy. In particular, he was shaken by the deaths, within the space of one year from 1970 to 1971, of three prominent rockers: Jimi Hendrix and singers Janis Joplin and Jim Morrison. Santana recalls: "All of a sudden playing pop music seemed strange. All the pop guys, like Jimi, Janis, and Jim Morrison, were dying left and right. It seemed to me that you either snorted cocaine and shot heroin or you folded your hands and thanked God. But I couldn't see myself in the streets, looking for someone to give me my fix."[53]

One of the changes Santana sought in his life concerned the direction of his music. The Santana band's sound had been wildly

The fatal drug overdoses of Doors lead singer Jim Morrison (facing camera) and other musicians inspired Santana to make positive changes in his life and music.

successful, and Columbia would have been happy to see him turning out more albums in a similar vein. But the guitarist was bored by the idea of simply repeating some tired formula indefinitely.

Fortunately, all three Santana albums were still selling well. The guitarist was under no great financial pressure to produce new material. He had the luxury of stretching out and experimenting.

This experimentation took him in several directions. One path was to make a series of guest appearances on other artists' albums. He collaborated in the early 1970s with Jefferson Airplane on their album *Bark* and on a solo album by Airplane violinist Papa John Creach. Other guest appearances included a shot on Brazilian pop-jazz singer Flora Purim's album *Stories to Tell*.

Santana also got together with a powerful singer and drummer, Buddy Miles. Miles was a veteran of the Electric Flag (a progressive blues band), Band of Gypsies (the group Hendrix formed late in his life), and his own band, the Buddy Miles Express. In the summer of 1972, Santana and Miles assembled a temporary band for a series of concerts. One of these gigs, at Diamond Head in Honolulu, Hawaii, was recorded and released as *Carlos Santana & Buddy Miles: Live!* Unfortunately, it was poorly received by critics, who felt that it was self-indulgent and sloppy, and its sales were also disappointing.

Back in the Studio

The guitarist's next studio album was the project that the Santana band had been working on when it broke up. Released in 1972 as *Caravanserai*, it did not list band members as a group. Instead, each track listed the individual musicians who contributed to it. This was a sure sign, if one was needed, that Santana, as a band with a fixed membership, no longer existed—but that Santana, the guitar player and bandleader, was very much present.

Several former members were also present. They included drummer Shrieve, who shared Santana's growing interest in spirituality and had remained friendly with the guitarist during the band's breakup. Also on hand for several cuts, as they had promised, were Rolie and Schon. These veterans were joined by a number of new faces, including saxophonist Hadley Caliman, keyboard players Rich Kermode and Tom Koster, and percussionists Armando Peraza and Rico Reyes.

Santana was happy to have some veterans from the band around for the sessions. He was exploring areas of music new to him, particularly jazz, and the task was daunting; the self-taught guitarist could not read music and felt self-conscious around musicians like Caliman, who were well-versed in the complexities of jazz. Santana was moving into the unknown.

Caravanserai

Caravanserai was, indeed, a bold departure for the guitarist. Although the album was intense in places like earlier albums, it varied greatly in mood from cut to cut. The guitarist was exploring ways to widen his instrument's possibilities; he remarks: "I wanted to understand how you could play one note and it could sound like the Pacific Ocean or another galaxy. How you could play a few notes and hear children, birds, bombs dropping."[54]

Santana was happy with *Caravanserai*, although the executives at Columbia were not sure that it would appeal to the buying public. Fortunately, their concerns were unfounded. *Caravanserai* produced no hit singles, and did not sell as massively as Santana's earlier albums, but it was still popular enough to reach a respectable number eight on the sales charts.

The album was also nominated for a Grammy Award, a sign that others in the recording industry held it in high esteem. Furthermore, critical attention was mostly positive. Praising the album, *Rolling Stone* magazine noted, "Carlos need never play another note to rank as one of the most satisfyingly beautiful players of his instrument, charming and moving melodic lines as the music swells and climaxes to swell again."[55]

"I Felt Like a Fake"

But musical experimentation was only one way in which Santana was moving in new directions. His interest in spiritual-

After his original band broke up, Santana achieved critical and popular success with his next album, Caravanserai.

"Only One Truth"

Santana speaks out frequently on the subjects of peace and music, which, to him, are closely intertwined. In this passage from an essay written to support a peace organization, the guitarist reflects on the topic:

There's only one truth on this planet: that we are all one. What I'd like to do before I die is bring people closer to . . . a reality of no borders, one race, one body —where we all take responsibility that nobody starves to death tomorrow morning. . . . When you connect with people through music, you affect the whole wheel of life in such a way that, even though you are only one person, you make a difference. . .

Music, more than almost anything else, has the power to bring people together people of different ages, races, religions. So I'm more clear now as to why I play. It's not just to make people happy or to make them dance— it's to change things: change myself, change the people in my band, change people all over the world, so we can have a clearer vision about life and about ourselves, so we can bring more harmony to the world.

Carlos Santana, "Carlos Santana Reflects on Working Toward Peace," *Architects of Peace*. www.scu.edu/ethics/architects-of-peace/Santana/essay.html.

ity, always strong, was growing intense. More than ever, he was becoming a seeker, looking for answers to life's mysteries.

Like many Latinos, Santana had been raised a Catholic, and that religion still had a strong hold on him. However, he discovered that it left him unfulfilled. More and more, he found himself drawn to Eastern religions—spiritual philosophies that had originated in Asia.

For a time, the guitarist was especially interested in the teachings of a well-known teacher from India, Paramahansa Yogananda. Teachers like Yogananda typically emphasize spiritual disciplines, including daily meditation and vegetarianism, as a means of keeping one's life pure. A path like Yogananda's struck Santana as a positive alternative to rock-star excess. He remarks: "After Woodstock, our egos got inflated. My life became more and more synthetic: I felt like a fake. All I care about is music, but I [started to get] pulled into the drugs, the parties. It was painful to lose my friends. I started meditating, seeking a new way."[56]

Meeting Mahavishnu

But Santana's interest in Yogananda did not last. In the early 1970s, he was introduced to another guru (spiritual leader) from India, one who would play a major part in the guitarist's life for several years. This was Sri Chinmoy.

Santana was introduced to Sri Chinmoy by John McLaughlin. McLaughlin was a blazingly fast, British-born guitarist who had made his name with several influential jazz-rock ensembles, including drummer Tony Williams's band, Lifetime, and Miles Davis's first electric bands. By the time Santana met him, McLaughlin was leading his own group, the Mahavishnu Orchestra.

Santana had heard the British guitarist on record, and they met for the first time in a New York City club where McLaughlin was performing. After the show, Santana introduced himself. The two hit it off personally and musically; they started spending time together, jamming whenever their paths crossed.

McLaughlin and his wife were both disciples of Sri Chinmoy and had officially changed their names to Mahavishnu and Mahalakshmi. McLaughlin's devotion to Sri Chinmoy resonated powerfully with Santana's own interest in spirituality, and the Indian teacher's philosophy offered what seemed to be a clear path of knowledge and faith. Simon Leng writes, "Sri Chinmoy was exactly what Carlos had been looking for at the time, a strong father figure to lead him away from the excesses of the rock life toward the search for inner fulfillment and spiritual peace."[57]

Meeting Deborah King

While Santana's friendship with McLaughlin was developing, the guitarist encountered someone else who would profoundly affect his life. This was Deborah King. A few years younger than Santana, she was a music fan, a college student, and the daughter of a professional blues guitarist, Saunders King.

Santana had been involved with many women over the years. But he has commented often that when he met Deborah King at a concert in early 1972, he knew right away that his bachelor days were over and that he had met his soul mate. A friend who was with Santana noticed it as well; he saw how the guitarist was looking at King and commented, "It's all over for you, man. That's the one."[58]

King was just as attracted to the tall, skinny, long-haired guitarist as he was to her. However, she was wary of his reputation as a womanizer. Furthermore, she had recently ended a stormy relationship with Sly Stone (of another well-known Bay Area band, Sly and the Family Stone), and she resisted the idea of going out with another celebrity.

British rocker John McLaughlin (pictured), who shared Santana's interest in Eastern religion, introduced Santana to spiritual leader Sri Chinmoy.

Marrying Deborah King

Santana had no such hesitation. He asked a mutual friend for her number, and despite her reservations, she agreed to go out. Their first date was to a concert by Azteca (a Latin-tinged band founded by former Santana percussionist Coke Escovedo); their next was dinner at a vegetarian restaurant, where they discovered a mutual interest in spirituality. After dinner, Santana took her to the Mill Valley home he shared with two cats, where they meditated and listened to John Coltrane.

The attraction proved strong and lasting; soon they were living together and King was joining him on tour whenever her studies permitted. In April 1973, they were married in a small ceremony at her uncle and aunt's house in Oakland. King's uncle, a minister, performed the service. The couple was so nervous that on the way there they took a wrong turn and were nearly late for their own wedding.

Santana and his wife, Deborah, shown here in 2006, met in 1972 and were married the following spring.

The occasion was not entirely joyous. Santana was still on such poor terms with his mother that he did not invite his parents. He had not even told them he was getting married; he was afraid that his forceful mother would have insisted on a formal church wedding.

Submitting to Sri Chinmoy

Like Carlos, Deborah was intensely spiritual but had, for some time, been pulling away from Western religion. Through the McLaughlins, she and Carlos were introduced to Sri Chinmoy himself. They attended several of his worship services in New York City and decided to become his disciples.

The couple adopted new names symbolic of their devotion. Carlos became Devadip and Deborah took the name Urmila. Devadip means "Lamp of God," "Eye of God," and "Light of God." Urmila means "Light of the Supreme."

In keeping with the teachings of their new spiritual leader, the couple changed other aspects of their lives as well. Carlos cut his hair short—a traumatic moment for both him and his wife—and began wearing all-white clothing; Deborah wore traditional, flowing Indian saris. They kept a strict vegetarian diet, swore off alcohol and drugs, and maintained a grueling schedule of work and meditation.

Constant, hard work was a cornerstone of Sri Chinmoy's philosophy. Under the guru's auspices, for example, Deborah opened and managed a vegetarian restaurant in San Francisco, one of several across the country operated by his disciples. It kept her busy all the time.

It was a difficult life, requiring a high degree of discipline and sacrifice. Santana comments, "It was like a West Point approach to spirituality."[59] His wife, who continued her longtime regimen of distance running, adds: "There was always this competition in how much we could do to prove our devotion—who could sleep the least and still function, because you were working so hard, how many miles could you run. I once ran a forty-seven-mile race. It wasn't enough just to run a marathon."[60]

The Turtle and the Hummingbird

Meanwhile, Santana diligently continued his music. Some outings were personal, barely commercial projects that he recorded as an aspect of his spiritual journey. One was the little-heard *Illuminations*, a duo with Turiya Alice Coltrane, the piano- and harp-playing widow of the intensely spiritual saxophonist John Coltrane.

It also seemed natural that he should record with McLaughlin. Their collaboration, *Love Devotion Surrender*, received mixed critical and popular reaction. Many felt that the album was full of blazing virtuosity but was low on meaningful emotion.

For Santana, it was intimidating to play with his friend McLaughlin, a virtuoso with a profound knowledge of jazz and music theory. At the same time, Santana realized the importance of understanding that "less is more," that a single precisely placed note can be more effective than a dozen ill-conceived ones. Comparing the experience of playing with McLaughlin to a turtle playing with a hummingbird, Santana comments: "I thought, 'Man, what am I going to do? I should just shine his shoes.' Then I found out that I may not play as many notes, or know as much as he does, but three notes—if you put them in the right place at the right time—are just as important."[61]

Uneven Music

The guitarist alternated these side projects with albums of more frankly commercial rock, recorded under the name Santana. He also toured regularly. In both cases, his band was an ever-rotating cast of backing musicians.

Santana continued to follow his musical instincts throughout the 1970s as popular taste picked up and dropped such musical fads and movements as disco and punk. Unfortunately, his albums were wildly uneven in terms of sales. For example, *Borboletta* peaked in the Top 20, but *Illuminations* barely made it into the Top 100.

The albums' musical quality was also uneven. They ranged from tepid jazz to unoriginal-sounding rock. Far more successful was a greatest hits album of surefire material that Columbia released in 1974.

More consistently successful were Santana's live tours, which regularly sold out across America, South America, Europe, and Asia. Concert audiences were always enthusiastic, and he toured relentlessly. This nearly nonstop schedule fit in well with Sri Chinmoy's admonitions to work constantly—Santana was gone more than he was home.

The Nose and the Heart

As of the mid-1970s, Santana's album sales were still disappointing. In 1975, hoping to improve them, the guitarist turned for advice to an old friend: Bill Graham, the manager who had been handling his business affairs, off an on, since the earliest days of the Santana Blues Band.

In Graham's opinion, the guitarist had erred in straying from his Latino roots—the musical genre that had first made him famous—and the manager urged a return. He suggested using David Rubinson—the same Columbia producer who had worked on the band's disastrous, unreleased first album. Santana was wary at first, but the two spoke and Santana decided that Rubinson was sincere.

Rubinson was eager to merge the two halves of the guitarist's musical personality—the aggressive rock of Santana with the quiet spirituality of Devadip. This was an issue that passionately interested the guitarist as well. He commented: "Santana is my nose, Devadip is my heart. My nose is still important because it's part of me. But what's [really] important is my heart."[62]

Santana's devotion to spiritual leader Sri Chinmoy led him to cut his long hair short, as seen in this 1975 photo.

The result of their collaboration was 1976's *Amigos*, which returned Santana to rock with a strong Latin influence. Its short, energetic, radio-friendly tunes were successful both artistically and in sales. Critics, who had been increasingly scornful of the guitarist's pallid efforts, applauded it as well.

Benefits

Naturally, Santana had a stake in making records that sold well. However, he was not hungry for a hit strictly for financial reasons. From his earliest successes, the guitarist had received good investment advice, and by now he was comfortably wealthy. He made music because he loved it and because he could use it to help others.

Santana thus frequently had time for nonprofit musical projects. For example, he often took part in devotional concerts dedicated to Sri Chinmoy. In contrast to his usual high-energy concerts, these were quiet, meditative affairs with acoustic instruments.

"A Certain Purity"

We thought it was appealing to the ear and to the soul. It made me feel good inside. There's a certain purity in the music that it seemed to recognize that would touch people if they really listened to it.

Drummer Michael Shrieve on *Caravanserai*, quoted in Simon Leng, *Soul Sacrifice: The Santana Story*, London: Firefly, 2000, p. 76.

Santana also put considerable energy into performing at benefit concerts. In 1973, for example, the guitarist joined the Rolling Stones for a concert to aid victims of a recent, devastating earthquake in Nicaragua. Another example was a free concert for the prisoners of California's Soledad Prison.

This mixture of activities, from quiet devotion and benefit concerts to out-and-out, round-the-world rocking, continued into the next phase of Santana's life. But in the following decades there would also be a new element: an intensely personal and heartrending look into the guitarist's own life history and psychological makeup.

Chapter 5

Holding Steady

The 1980s and 1990s were decades of conflict for Santana. In part, this unsettled feeling was caused by the split between Santana's gentle, spiritual half and his fierce, rock-star half; it created a tension that the guitarist found increasingly intolerable. He reflects: "For a long time, I felt I was at war. The Santana thing was on one side and the Devadip thing was on the other."[63]

Related to this, he and Deborah were increasingly dissatisfied with their spiritual path. As a result, in the early 1980s they drew away from Sri Chinmoy. The couple had once embraced the spiritual leader wholeheartedly, and they still felt that he had provided much that was good for them. However, more and more they were chafing under his guidance.

"Old Tennis Shoes"

One aspect of Sri Chinmoy's regimen that they found especially difficult was his insistence that followers devote themselves to him alone, wholly and unquestioningly. Carlos and Deborah were beginning to believe that there were many paths to enlightenment; in their opinion, Sri Chinmoy was only one of many

Disenchanted with the demands of Sri Chinmoy, Santana (shown here in 1976) and his wife, Deborah, broke ties with the guru.

possible connections to the spiritual life. As Deborah notes in her memoir, *Space Between the Stars*, "Carlos and I had outgrown his [Sri Chinmoy's] make-believe realm and had unbraided our mental dependency on him as our link to God."[64]

The couple also felt that the ultra-strict lifestyle the guru advocated was counterproductive. Deborah notes that Sri Chinmoy's spiritual regimen, instead of increasing the love around her, was actually destroying her family. In part, this was because of the heavy work ethic. In theory, the practice of non-stop work created maximum spiritual awareness by isolating followers from the world's distractions; in practice, it meant that families were constantly separated.

Another problem was the guru's insistence that Deborah avoid having children. Sri Chinmoy's justification for this was that children only distracted one from the rigorous path of spiritual awareness. And yet Deborah yearned to start a family.

All in all, Carlos and Deborah felt that they needed to change in ways that life under Sri Chinmoy did not allow. Or, perhaps, they simply outgrew him. Carlos comments, "After a while I began to look at it like my old tennis shoes from Mission High School that didn't fit me anymore."[65]

Rejoining Christianity, Sort Of

When the Santanas made the painful decision to leave the guru's tight grasp, they hoped to make it an amicable split. But the spiritual leader tried hard to keep them, telling them that their spiritual awareness would lapse disastrously without him. "He was pretty vindictive for a while," Carlos later said. "He told all my friends not to call me ever again, because I was to drown in the dark sea of ignorance for leaving him."[66]

In the wake of their messy "divorce" from the spiritual leader, Deborah took the lead in the Santanas' religious life. She reembraced Christianity and began going to church regularly. Carlos joined his wife in this—in part, at least, simply to make her happy. He comments, "I became a born-again Christian to appease her, so to speak."[67]

But the guitarist's spiritual beliefs continued to extend far beyond traditional Christianity. The faith Santana embraces, he has often said, has no easy label or particular name. He muses: "Any religion that judges and condemns is a spiritually retarded religion. . . . One that brings kindness and redemption—a win-win situation for people and the planet—that's my religion."[68]

Starting a Family

After splitting with Sri Chinmoy, there were immediate changes in the Santanas' life together. One was the amount of time they spent together. Previously, Carlos had been gone for months at a time, and when at home was a night owl who frequented clubs or practiced until late at night. Deborah, meanwhile, got up early every morning, was busy at the restaurant all day, and was so exhausted that she could barely stay awake in the evenings.

After the split, however, the couple rediscovered the pleasure of each other's company. They spent long periods enjoying their life together at home. They also traveled extensively—sometimes just for fun, sometimes on tour.

Their lives changed in other ways as well. They dressed in normal clothes again and even ate meat on occasion. Deborah writes: "I remember ordering my first chicken sandwich in Spain. It was so delicious."[69]

A more profound change was the growth of their family. A son, Salvador, was born in 1983, and two daughters, Stella and Angelica, arrived soon after. In 1987, the Santanas found a larger house, in the Marin County town of San Rafael, to accommodate the new additions.

After severing connections with Sri Chinmoy's philosophies, Santana pursued other spiritual paths.

Santana was delighted to be a father. He slowed down his touring and recording schedule dramatically so that he was able to spend more time at home with his family. Typical of this slower pace was his schedule for 1986: He played fewer than thirty concerts. In terms of touring, it was his lightest year in twenty years as a rock guitarist.

"School Is Out, Let's Play"

Santana did not stop performing entirely, of course. This was in part simply because he loved it; but continued music making also meant continued financial stability for his growing family. Among the tours he did undertake during this period were a couple of highly successful excursions with two other rock legends, Bob Dylan and British guitarist Jeff Beck. Santana also continued to guest star on albums by such artists as Weather Report, soul diva Aretha Franklin, and blues legend John Lee Hooker.

Bikers, Hippies, and Grandmothers

No other performer attracts bikers, former hippies, middle-class Hispanics, Chicanos . . . lovers of Latin jazz, blacks, curious white college students, whole families from babies to grandmothers.

Writer Pete Warshal, quoted in Steve Heilig, "Carlos Santana: An Interview with Steve Heilig," *Whole Earth,* Summer 2000. www.wholeearthmag.com/Article Bin/375.html.

Two of these guest shots were recordings with a pair of very different singers with Latino roots: José Feliciano and Leon Patillo. Patillo was especially delighted to have the guitarist on board. He recalls, "I was so honoured and privileged to have him on my album, when he walked into the studio you could see the smile on my face a block away."[70]

With his own recordings, Santana worked in an even greater variety of styles than before. In large part, this reflected the sense of freedom he felt after leaving the austerity of Sri Chinmoy's discipline. The guitarist says: "It was like, 'School is out, let's play. Let's experiment!' I was just learning how to have fun again."[71]

More Recordings

One result of this newfound sense of freedom was *Swing of Delight*, a jazz-fusion album featuring such top-flight performers as pianist Herbie Hancock, saxophonist Wayne Shorter, and bassist Ron Carter. Another was a record of loose, danceable rock, *Zebop!* This album was a deliberate attempt to have a commercial hit; Santana said at the time: "We want a new audience. I want to reach more people . . . and not sound like an antique."[72]

Zebop! succeeded in this; compared to Santana's other recordings of the period, it was a big success. It generated a Top 20 single, "Winning," and the album itself reached the Top Ten. Its follow-up, *Shango*, gave Santana his first Top Ten single in more than a decade, "Hold On." *Shango* also reunited Santana with his old bandmate Gregg Rolie; despite this powerful combination, however, *Shango* sold surprisingly poorly.

The guitarist and Rolie hit it off so well during their reunion in the studio that they made tentative plans to form a new band, to be called Friends Again. The new group would have used the current bass player from Santana and the drummer from Rolie's band, Journey—but no Latin percussion. Friends Again progressed only as far as cutting a few demonstration tapes before the idea was dropped. The drummer, Steve Smith, recalls, "It was a good idea, but needed a lot of work."[73]

Musical Ups and Downs

Another high spot of this period was one of Santana's personal favorites among his many albums: *Blues for Salvador*, a mostly instrumental set released in 1987. Though it did not sell in huge numbers, critics praised the album, and it received strong airplay on jazz stations. Furthermore, the title piece won a Grammy Award for best rock instrumental performance.

Mixed in with such commercially successful recordings like *Zebop!* and artistically satisfying albums like *Blues for Salvador* were many that fared poorly. *Havana Moon*, for example, sank without a trace despite the presence of such heavyweight guests as singer Willie Nelson, organist-singer Booker T. Jones, and a great Texas blues-rock band, the Fabulous Thunderbirds.

Part of the problem was a growing antagonism between Santana and his record company, Columbia. The label had fired its president, Clive Davis, and the label's new executives focused almost exclusively on profits. They wanted tried-and-true commercial music and were less tolerant of Santana's more eccentric or experimental projects.

Although he continued to perform, Santana reduced his touring schedule after his children were born.

Another Disappointment

Some of the blame for Santana's weak sales can certainly be attributed to the uneven quality of his output. Santana, however, faulted the record company; he complained that the new executives ignored him, promoted his records poorly, and refused to issue his best material. For example, Columbia refused to release a live album drawn from promising tapes of Santana's tour with Wayne Shorter.

Another disappointment for Santana during this period was his work on the soundtrack for *La Bamba*. This was a fictionalized biographical movie of early Latino rock-and-roll star Ritchie Valens. (Valens was one of the rockers who died in the 1959 plane crash that also killed singer-guitarist Buddy Holly.) Santana enjoyed working with gifted, creative musicians like rockers Los Lobos and blues pioneer Willie Dixon. However, he had difficulty dealing with the film industry. He recalls: "It was

Lou Diamond Phillips (pictured) portrayed early rock musician Ritchie Valens in the 1987 movie La Bamba. *Santana worked on the soundtrack for the film.*

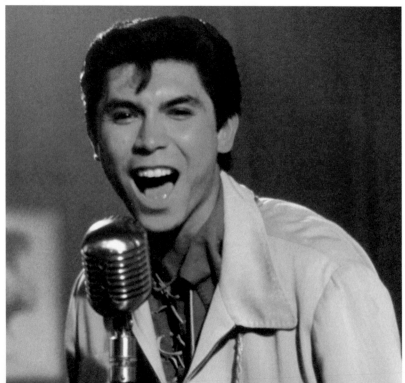

really frustrating because of the egos that are involved in making movies. . . . The Hollywood machine is very insensitive to people's souls."[74]

Big Concerts

One bright spot in Santana's career during this period was the continued presence in the band of a gifted keyboardist, Chester Thompson. Thompson (not to be confused with a drummer of the same name who played briefly with Santana) was with another top Bay Area band, Tower of Power, until he joined Santana in 1983. The two would form a close playing and songwriting union for the next decade.

Other bright spots in this period included several high-profile concert appearances. One was a major concert benefiting Amnesty International. Another was the Live Aid show in 1985—the largest charity concert ever held. Live Aid was a sixteen-hour marathon held simultaneously in Philadelphia and London to benefit famine victims in Ethiopia. It starred, in addition to Santana, luminaries like U2, Queen, Madonna, Elton John, Phil Collins, Sting, and Eric Clapton.

In 1986, on the twentieth anniversary of the formation of the original Santana Blues Band, the guitarist organized a reunion concert with as many members as possible from over the years. A total of seventeen former and current Santana musicians took to the stage in various combinations. The only member of every group was Santana himself.

The reunion went so well that in 1988 the guitarist organized a tour with some of the original players. Besides Santana himself, the band included Rolie, Shrieve, and Areas. The lineup was rounded out by three newer additions: Thompson, bassist Alphonso Johnson, and percussionist Armando Peraza. This reunion tour was a success financially and personally—everyone had fun.

A New Label

Unfortunately, Santana's relations with Columbia finally grew too rancorous. Following the exceptionally poor sales of 1990's *Spirits Dancing in the Flesh*, the record company and Santana parted ways after twenty-two years. The guitarist made his dissatisfaction clear at the time: "I just couldn't stay any longer, now . . . it's all quantity and no quality."[75]

The following year, Santana signed with Polydor Records, which promised him complete creative control and gave him his own custom label, Guts and Grace. (The name was suggested by Shorter to symbolize Santana's combination of passion and serenity.) Under this label, Santana was slated to release live recordings from his collection by Hendrix, Davis, Coltrane, and other musical legends.

The first album for the new company, *Milagro*, had a melancholy tone. This likely reflected Carlos's grief over the recent death, in a helicopter crash, of his longtime friend and manager, Bill Graham. Deborah notes, "Bill had been a brother and father to Carlos."[76]

Not a Band

[The reunion band] wasn't what I hoped it would be, it wasn't a band. It was like Carlos bringing in some guys from the original band and then proceeding as a band leader. I was frustrated, I had high hopes, but it was not a band anymore.

Drummer Michael Shrieve, quoted in Simon Leng, *Soul Sacrifice: The Santana Story*. London: Firefly, 2000, p. 150–51.

Milagro was followed by a live set (*Sacred Fire—Live in South America*) and by *Santana Brothers*, a trio outing featuring his brother Jorge Santana and their nephew, Carlos Hernandez. Both albums received mixed reviews and did mediocre business, although some prestigious critics continued to praise Santana. Typical of these was the review of *Milagro* in *Musician* magazine, which raved: "Awesome. Santana's guitar playing remains clear-eyed and invigorating."[77]

A Rough Patch Personally

These recordings failed to revive Santana's track record, but sluggish sales were not the guitarist's only worries. His private life was also in flux during this period. One bad time came in 1991, when Santana was arrested for the first time in his life. He

Santana poses at the Mountain Aire Festival in Sonora, California, in 1987.

was stopped and searched at a Houston, Texas, airport and authorities found a small amount of marijuana.

The guitarist was released on bail, and when the case was heard later that year the charge was reduced to a misdemeanor, because it was Santana's first offense and the amount of marijuana was small. His only punishment was a fine of one hundred dollars, although he was also required to make some antidrug public service announcements.

Far more serious were problems between Santana and his wife. Back in 1978, Deborah had discovered that Carlos was having an ongoing affair with a musician who lived in the Bay Area. Despite Carlos's heartfelt pleas for her to stay, she had moved in with her sister for three months before they reconciled. Now, in the early 1990s, Deborah found out that Carlos was still having brief affairs whenever he was on the road. She confronted him and he promised to stop.

Meanwhile, despite his reputation as a normally gentle, sweet person, the guitarist's temper and mood had been growing steadily worse. This was perhaps a reflection of his stagnant career and his long-brewing dissatisfaction with the recording industry. Santana reflects: "I was very much thinking like a victim. I was angry, bitter, disillusioned. For a while I felt lost in a creative way."[78]

Facing His Secret

As Carlos grew steadily more angry and depressed, Deborah worried that the marriage might not be able to continue, and she urged him to see a therapist. Out of those therapy sessions in the mid-1990s came a startling revelation, a terrible memory that Carlos had suppressed for decades. He had been molested as a child.

This abuse had occurred when he lived in Tijuana. It lasted for about two years, when he was ten to twelve years old. As he remembered it, an American who dressed like a cowboy made friends with him.

The American would bring Carlos across the border to the States, buy him presents, and sexually assault him. The guitarist says: "I was seduced by toys, and I was seduced by being brought to America with all kinds of gifts and stuff. And, being a child, I blocked that other part, because there was the other goodies."[79]

The abuse ended when Carlos started being attracted to girls. The American, finding Carlos looking at a girl, jealously hit him. Carlos realized that he was in the company of a sick man, and he avoided the "cowboy" after that. The experience was so traumatic that he put it away in a corner of his mind and consciously forgot about it.

"Burn All Those Things, Man"

However, with therapy—and the support of his family—Santana found the strength to bring the problem into the light and work through the issues it raised. He says now that the entire experience, though painful, helped him become more creative: "I have learned to convert all this [negative] energy now into something productive and creative. . . . It's just fuel now. You use it to do something creative."[80]

Santana, always an intensely private man, vowed at first to keep the story of his abuse secret. However, the guitarist went public with the story after a few years, realizing that talking about it might help or inspire others. He revealed his story in a 2000 *Rolling Stone* magazine interview and on the television show *60 Minutes II*. He stated:

> There's a lot of people out there who have this kind of
> pain and anguish, and [it's good] if you show your face

In the hope of helping other victims, Santana publicly discussed the sexual abuse he had suffered as a child.

and say, "I am healed. I can be healed.". . . You don't have to ruin the rest of your life and ruin your family's life by blaming yourself, feeling dirty, ashamed. Burn all those things, man. Burn all those things in a letter, burn it, take the ashes, plant some roses and put the ashes on it, and watch it grow. And let it go.[81]

All Over?

Santana blames the abuse, and the shame and guilt it created in his mind, for the anger and depression he experienced. "The mind has a very insidious way of making you feel guilty," he commented in the *Rolling Stone* interview. "You're the guilty party, shame on you, you're the one who brought this on yourself. . . . All the times I was angry with the original band or with my wife, till '95, it was all of that."[82]

The therapy sessions helped Santana smooth out many of the rough areas in his personal life. However, the guitarist found himself at another crossroads at the end of the 1990s. He was still a top draw on the concert circuit, but his record sales remained stagnant.

In fact, they were so poor that Polydor did not re-sign him when his contract came up for renewal. Santana was without a recording contract for the first time since he had originally signed with Columbia. To many in the music industry, it looked like Santana's time was over—that he was a relic of another era, his best years behind him. Deborah Santana writes: "Carlos's sound was recognized everywhere in the world, his unique guitar sound undisputed—but music [had become] an industry of numbers, Top 40 hits, payola [bribery], and luck. It was not the sixties anymore."[83]

Many observers predicted that the guitarist would never pull out of this fallow period. But they were wrong—spectacularly so. Santana's fortunes were about to change, as he reinvented himself for a new generation.

Chapter 6

Renewal

Carlos Santana recorded for two other labels, Island and EMI, after Polydor. Neither was a good fit, however. This lack of a permanent home finally ended when Deborah Santana urged her husband toward a promising new option.

This was Arista Records. Arista was a relatively new label headed by Clive Davis, who had been president of Columbia during the Santana band's glory years. Davis and the guitarist were long-time friends and had enjoyed a close working relationship.

The two met in Los Angeles to discuss the possibility of Santana signing with Arista. Davis asked the guitarist what he wanted to do with his music, and Santana replied, in his typically abstract way, that he wanted to use music to reconnect the molecules with the light. Davis took this answer in stride, Santana recalls: "He wasn't fazed. He could have said, 'Uh-oh, here's a far-out hippie.'"[84]

The Timeless Santana Sound

Instead of recoiling, Davis enthusiastically offered Santana a contract. The record executive was aware of the guitarist's

79

An Outspoken Pioneer

Santana's current status as an elder statesman of rock has allowed him to reflect on, among other things, the world of Latin pop and his place in it. He views the current wave of interest in Latin music as generally positive, although he is wary of its faddish aspects. In his opinion, it is partly artificial—an invented product of the music industry, rather than a valid, organic artistic form. In a 1999 interview, he commented: "The Latin-explosion thing, a lot of it is media hype. . . . They [music industry executives] are into exploiting; I am into exploring. . . . People are going crazy with the Latin frenzy and the Spanish frenzy, but it is really African music that Ricky Martin is playing and Jennifer Lopez is playing and I'm playing."

Quoted in David Wild, "Cosmic Carlos," *Rolling Stone*, August 19, 1999.

Musician Ricky Martin presents Santana with the Legend Award at the 2005 World Music Awards held in Los Angeles.

decades of mediocre sales and near-neglect. However, he also saw a chance to stage a major comeback for his friend.

In Davis's opinion, the engine to drive this comeback would be an album capitalizing on the then-growing wave of interest in Latin pop. This interest was typified by such smash hits as Ricky Martin's "La Vida Loca." Simon Leng notes:

> Davis is a very astute businessman and it had not escaped his notice that Spanish was already [a primary] language of many American states and that a new teenage Hispanic heartthrob called Ricky Martin had crossed over to the mainstream charts with a smash hit single. Carlos Santana was still a name without peer in the Latin community and Davis knew that if they could target a single at the huge Hispanic audience, sales would soar.[85]

The music executive imagined that such an album would combine two worlds. It would have the classic, timeless Santana sound, but it would also have astutely chosen elements of up-to-the-minute pop—an area of music the guitarist was already keenly aware of. Davis reflects, "We knew half had to be vintage Santana, but that we also had to incorporate all of the current contemporary influences that Carlos was very much feeling."[86]

Duets

To fuse these two elements, Davis suggested an album of duets with guest singers. Each of these performers would sing and write a song. Each track would be a potential hit single.

This formula—pairing a seasoned performer with guest performers from a younger generation—was not new. It had been successfully used before with legends like Frank Sinatra and Ray Charles. Sometimes the pairings were questionable—Sinatra's duet with Bono is often cited as a particularly poor choice. But frequently it worked beautifully, reviving a vintage sound and making it work for a new generation of fans.

Davis, whose hit-making instincts had been accurate many times before, was convinced that the format would work for

Santana. The guitarist agreed that, if done intelligently, the melding of old and new would make his music both familiar and fresh. Santana remarks: "I didn't want . . . to sound like a Seventies jukebox. I wanted to be relevant today or as Wayne Shorter would say, 'Completely new, totally familiar.'"[87]

Cooking with Carlos

Many musicians were approached in the early stage of the project. An important consideration, when inviting potential performers, was that they already appreciated Santana's style. Davis wanted to avoid clashes with performers who were incompatible or unfamiliar with the classic Santana sound.

An all-star list of singers, rappers, and musicians was assembled, among them, Wyclef Jean, Lauryn Hill (on whose *Miseducation* album Santana had recently guest starred), Rob Thomas of Matchbox 20, Eagle-Eye Cherry, Everlast, Eric Clapton, and Dave Matthews.

Many of these performers already had songs in hand when they arrived to work with the legendary guitarist. An exception was Dave Matthews, who collaborated with Santana to write the haunting "Love of My Life." As did the other guests, Matthews had a wonderful time. He comments: "Hanging out with Carlos was really enlightening. Even though he's such a heavyweight, he's an incredibly kind man. Recording with him was like being away at a retreat as opposed to going to work."[88]

Santana enthusiastically joined in with the collaborative process of making *Supernatural*, as the album was eventually called. It was a new experience for him. Although for decades he had been calling the shots, the guitarist willingly gave up an unprecedented amount of artistic control.

In return, he trusted that Davis, his production team, and his musical collaborators could, together with the guitarist, produce something both commercially satisfying and artistically nourishing. It was like sharing a kitchen with a gifted cook, Santana comments: "I tell you, it's the most incidental I've ever felt on an album. You walk in like a chef. The water's boiling, the garlic's happening, the onions are in. And you just cook."[89]

Rob Thomas and Santana, who collaborated on the 1999 album Supernatural, *perform in Beverly Hills, California, in 2006.*

The First Singles

With this spirit of collaboration strong in the studio, the recording was swift and enjoyable. Once it was complete, everyone remained enthusiastic about the possibilities of the album. And when the album was released in midsummer 1999, this enthusiasm proved to be well-placed; everything about *Supernatural* was a stunning success.

The song chosen as the album's first single was "Smooth," cowritten and sung by Rob Thomas. It was an instant hit with music directors at radio stations that played a wide variety of musical styles. As a result, people representing a broad spectrum of listening habits started hearing "Smooth."

And they liked it. The song shot to number one on the sales charts and stayed there for an impressive twelve weeks. The follow-up single, "Maria Maria," with arranger Bobby Martin, was nearly as successful, spending ten weeks at the top of the charts.

Another Shot at "La Vida Loca"

The album, meanwhile, was also a phenomenon. It debuted at number one and stayed there for six weeks, a remarkably long time in the fickle world of pop music. By the end of the year, it had sold 4 million copies. It has since sold well over 22 million copies in the United States alone. (In stark contrast to this was the previous Santana album, which had sold only about two hundred thousand.)

By a huge margin, and by any standard, *Supernatural* was Santana's biggest commercial success. It proved popular with the critics as well. Typical was the response of *Rolling Stone* magazine; its reviewer, David Wild, commented:

Santana was part of the pre-game show that kicked off the 2003 Super Bowl in San Diego, California.

It's been too long since Carlos Santana delivered a new studio album worthy of his awesome gifts, and for whatever reasons, all the high-profile attention he receives here appears to have reinvigorated his muse. Eclectic, lively and only occasionally goofy, *Supernatural* offers a glossy but winning context of musical fusion that highlights Santana's unique ability to make that guitar of his cry expressively. . . . Who could begrudge such an enduring guitar god another big, star-studded shot at living *la vida loca*?[90]

The Big Comeback

At the 2000 Grammy Awards ceremony, *Supernatural* was the heavyweight contender. It swept the event, receiving eleven nominations and winning nine, including album of the year and song of the year (for "Smooth"). Then, at the Latin Grammy Awards ceremony later that year, *Supernatural* picked up another three awards. In the eyes of everyone—the buying public, the critics, other artists, and the recording industry, which presents the Grammys—Carlos Santana was the comeback story of the year.

Santana was delighted and grateful, of course, for the album's commercial success, and for his amazing comeback as a force in the music industry. But it was clearly not just about money for him. The guitarist also recognized that his success pointed to something more significant—that the album's multigenerational appeal could have a positive effect on his audience. He comments:

> When you consider the phenomenon of "Supernatural," it's the first album in a long time that parents, grandchildren and kids got into. Usually, parents and teen-agers don't listen to the same thing, so "Supernatural" is quite a phenomenon. And that really validated the direction; it really confirmed that what we're doing with our music is the right thing.[91]

Honors

Supernatural and the amazing comeback story it created solidified Santana's role as the premiere figure in Latin rock and an enduring guitar hero. To many observers, the multiple awards *Supernatural* picked up were long overdue. But these awards have been, by no means, the only honors Santana has received over the years.

For example, in 1987, San Francisco declared a "Santana Day," highlighted by a free concert in the streets. In 1996, the guitarist received a star on the Hollywood Rock Walk of Fame. And in 1998, the "classic" Santana band was inducted into the Rock and Roll Hall of Fame.

The guitarist was also honored in 2000 in his former home of Tijuana, where he was given the keys to the city and named Tijuana's cultural ambassador. His hometown of Autlán has named a street in his honor. And in 2004, he was the Latin Recording Academy Person of the Year. Furthermore, early in 2005, he became a BMI Icon. (BMI is an organization that oversees music performing rights.) He joined such music legends as James Brown, Brian Wilson, Al Green, Chuck Berry, Dolly Parton, Isaac Hayes, and Van Morrison in accepting this honor.

Informal tributes to the guitarist also abound. The many fan-based Web sites devoted to him are perhaps one sure sign of enduring fame. Murals featuring the guitarist have also appeared here and there over the years. One of these, by artist Michael Rios, is in San Francisco's Mission District, Santana's home during his lean years. The mural honors Santana and several other Latin music giants.

More Music

In the years after *Supernatural*'s release, Santana followed its runaway success with more albums that used a similar format: guest stars and short, punchy songs with strong Latin overtones. In 2002, *Shaman* paired the guitarist with, among others, P.O.D., Seal, Macy Gray, and even opera superstar Plácido Domingo. In 2005 came *All That I Am*, featuring Steven Tyler, Michelle Branch, Big Boi, Joss Stone, and many more. In each case, Santana's pithy guitar solos shared the spotlight equally with the vocals (and, to some ears, were often superior).

Neither *Shaman* nor *All That I Am* had the runaway success of *Supernatural*. However, both sold extremely well. A number of singles also fared well, particularly "The Game of Love," with Michelle Branch, which won a Grammy Award for best pop collaboration with vocals.

Meanwhile, Santana has continued to guest star on other artists' albums. For example, in 2005, jazz pianist Herbie Hancock—an old friend and another longtime San Francisco–area resident—asked the guitarist to help him enlist artists for *Possibilities*, an album similar in spirit to *Supernatural*. In addition to these recruiting duties, Santana performed on "Safiatou" alongside singer Angélique Kidjo.

Good Causes

Thanks to the triumph in recent years of *Supernatural* and its successors, Santana has been able to amplify something he has always done: donating his time and money. Ever since his first financial successes, the guitarist had contributed generously to humanitarian causes, either in cash donations or by appearing at benefit concerts. *Supernatural* and its follow-ups simply gave him greater financial clout than before.

To focus their donations, the guitarist and his wife, an active partner in his philanthropy, founded the Milagro Foundation in 1998. (*Milagro* is Spanish for "miracle.") To date, this foundation has given out some $2 million in grants to humanitarian agencies, with a special emphasis on groups that help children in need.

As part of honors he received in his home-town of Autlán, Mexico, Santana made a cast of his hands in a cement block.

The foundation has sometimes responded to one-time crises, such as donating to the families of firefighters killed in the 9/11 attacks and to victims of the 2004 Asian tsunami. But it has also focused much of its giving on agencies with longer-range goals. Among those benefiting have been such groups as the Hispanic Education and Media Group, Doctors Without Borders, Save the Children, Childreach, Rainforest Action Network, Greenpeace, American Indian College Fund, Amnesty International, and the Museum of Tolerance.

The Santanas have devised a number of ways to raise money for humanitarian causes. Some of these have been lighthearted; for example, they have designed lines of women's shoes, as well as fragrances for men and women. The profits from these enterprises go directly into the foundation. A more traditional example was that all of the proceeds from Santana's 2003 American tour went toward the fight against the AIDS pandemic in South Africa.

The Milagro Foundation has received a number of honors for its work. For example, in March 2006, it was honored at the annual Tequio Awards. These awards are presented by California Rural Legal Assistance, an organization that fights for farmworkers and other needy Latinos.

Speaking Out

Just as he is willing financially to support causes close to his heart, Santana is also willing to speak out on issues. For example, he has been vocal about his belief that education should be taught bilingually, in both English and Spanish, in areas of the United States with large Latino populations.

Sometimes, Santana's strongly held opinions are politically or personally inconvenient. For example, twice during the 1990s, the guitarist was invited by President Bill Clinton to perform at White House galas. Santana liked Clinton personally and generally agreed with his policies, but he turned the invitations down because he disliked the civil rights records of the South American dignitaries he would have entertained.

Similarly, Santana backed out of doing music for a Hispanic-themed television show, "AKA Pablo," because he felt the characters were stereotyped. (The show ran for one season in the mid-1980s.) And the guitarist initially refused an invitation to play at a second Woodstock festival in 1994 because most of the acts were white; he relented after a number of African American performers were added.

Santana has continued to be politically outspoken. In March 2006, the guitarist criticized President George W. Bush's aggressive policy in Iraq, invoking the words of a longtime hero. Santana told reporters: "My concept is the opposite of George W. Bush. . . . There is more value in placing a flower in a rifle barrel than making war. As Jimi Hendrix used to say, musical notes have more importance than bullets."[92]

At Home

Santana's personal life in recent years has slowed down somewhat. This is not due to age; even as he nears sixty, he is still healthy and energetic enough to tour and create music constantly. "I haven't

Santana greets fans at an Oakland Raiders football game in October 2003.

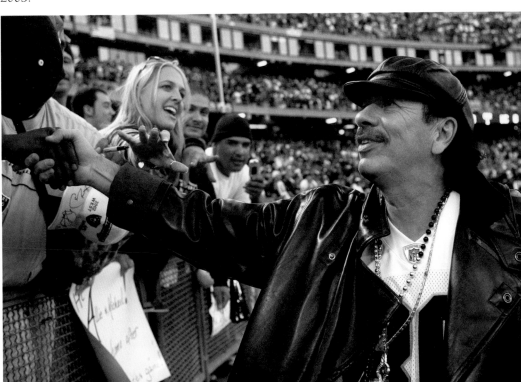

reached that point [of retiring]," he comments. "I'm too much involved in discovering notes every day. There's only so many notes but, to me, each one is like an ocean."[93]

The guitarist used to tour nonstop, and sometimes was gone for most of the year. As their family grew, however, Deborah Santana laid down some firm rules for her husband. Any time spent on the road had to be balanced with an equal amount of time at home. Furthermore, when he is at home, Deborah has always made sure that Carlos participates fully in family life. She says: "When he comes home, I don't want to hear about Carlos Santana. I want him to hear about the children, I want him to take over some of the responsibility. I'll warn him: 'Remember, when you come home, you are a father. There is recycling to be done, you're going to be driving the car pool.' Because that's my reality."[94]

The Church

Santana's business matters—maintaining the band organization, running the charitable foundation, keeping the fan club current—are handled in offices in an industrial park in San Rafael, about twenty minutes north of San Francisco. A few minutes' drive away is the home the family has maintained for many years.

The Santanas' private property includes two buildings: the family's house and a second structure up a small hill. The guitarist calls this building his church. It may be the only church in the world that houses a vintage Spider-Man pinball machine on the second floor.

Santana and his wife, Deborah, shown here in New York City in 2005, strive to maintain a balance between public life and family life.

Despite the presence of such lighthearted touches, the building has a serious purpose; it is a combination practice space, listening room, and meditation sanctuary. Santana can practice or listen to music there, even late at night, without bothering others. And it is a place for communing with his heroes, the guitarist comments: "Here's where I hang out with Jimi and Miles and whoever, and play and meditate."[95]

Angels

As its name suggests, Santana's church is his favored meditation spot. When he meditates, which is daily, he sits in front of the fireplace and faces the wall with lit candles around him. He keeps a yellow legal pad at one side, ready for the communications that he hopes will come from angels: "It's kind of like a fax machine."[96]

Santana has been interested in angels since the late 1980s, when he first became involved with a group that claimed to channel them. One member of this group said that before the making of *Supernatural*, an angel named Metatron had contacted him, predicting that Santana would soon be heard everywhere.

Santana has remarked that he has personally also received instructions from Metatron. The guitarist says, for instance, that messages received while recording *Supernatural* inspired him to make it appeal to several generations. He says that such direct contact with an angel is an amazing experience: "It's an enormous peace, the few times I have felt the presence in the room. I feel lit up. I'm not Carlos anymore, I'm not bound to DNA anymore. It's beyond sex, it's beyond anything that in this world could give you a buzz. It makes me feel like Jesus embraced me and I'm bathed in light."[97]

Such statements make it clear that Santana remains an eager spiritual seeker, an aspect of his personality that surely helps him stay young in spirit. His deep desire to continue creating new music has also helped keep his heart young. Santana will no doubt remain active and vital for years to come, a hero to millions and one of the world's most important and influential Latino musicians.

Notes

Introduction: The Guitarist

1. Quoted in BrainyQuote, "Carlos Santana Quotes." www.brainyquote.com/quotes/authors/c/carlos_santana. html.
2. Quoted in Simon Leng, *Soul Sacrifice: The Santana Story.* London: FireFly, 2000, p. 172.
3. Quoted in David Wild, "Cosmic Carlos," *Rolling Stone,* August 19, 1999.
4. Quoted in Marc Shapiro, *Carlos Santana: Back on Top.* New York: St. Martin's, 2000, p. 4.
5. Quoted in Chris Heath, "The Epic Life of Carlos Santana," *Rolling Stone,* March 16, 2000.
6. Carlos Santana, "Carlos Santana Reflects on Working Toward Peace," Architects of Peace. www.scu.edu/ethics/ architects-of-peace/Santana/essay.html.

Chapter 1: From Jalisco to San Francisco

7. Quoted in Leng, *Soul Sacrifice,* p. 12.
8. Quoted in Shapiro, *Carlos Santana,* pp. 15–16.
9. Quoted in Leng, *Soul Sacrifice,* p. 12.
10. Quoted in Steve Heilig, "Carlos Santana: An Interview with Steve Heilig," *Whole Earth,* Summer 2000. www. wholeearthmag.com/ArticleBin/375.html.
11. Quoted in Santanamigos, 1947–1966. http://perso. wanadoo.fr/santanamigos/1947.htm.
12. Quoted in Shapiro, *Carlos Santana,* p. 16.
13. Quoted in Heilig, "Carlos Santana."
14. Quoted in Heilig, "Carlos Santana."
15. Quoted in "Santana." www.loveandromance.com/features/ get-features.asp?id=342&catid=17.
16. Quoted in "Santana."
17. Quoted in Leng, *Soul Sacrifice,* p. 16.
18. Quoted in Heath, "The Epic Life of Carlos Santana."

19. Quoted in Heilig, "Carlos Santana."
20. Quoted in Heilig, "Carlos Santana."
21. Quoted in Santanamigos, 1947–1966.
22. Quoted in Heath, "The Epic Life of Carlos Santana."
23. Quoted in Leng, *Soul Sacrifice*, p. 25.
24. Quoted in Deborah Santana, *Space Between the Stars.* New York: Ballantine, 2005, p. 134.
25. Quoted in Santana, *Space Between the Stars*, p. 207.
26. Quoted in Santana, *Space Between the Stars*, p. 130.

Chapter 2: The Santana Blues Band
27. Quoted in Relix, "Carlos Santana," September 2005. http://perso.wanadoo.fr/santanamigos/menu.htm.
28. Quoted in Heilig, "Carlos Santana."
29. Quoted in Shapiro, *Carlos Santana*, p. 71.
30. Quoted in Heath, "The Epic Life of Carlos Santana."
31. Quoted in Heath, "The Epic Life of Carlos Santana."
32. Quoted in Heath, "The Epic Life of Carlos Santana."
33. Quoted in Shapiro, *Carlos Santana*, pp. 69–70.
34. Quoted in Heath, "The Epic Life of Carlos Santana."
35. Quoted in Shapiro, *Carlos Santana*, p. 67.
36. Quoted in Shapiro, *Carlos Santana*, p. 68.
37. Quoted in Shapiro, *Carlos Santana*, p. 74.
38. Leng, *Soul Sacrifice*, p. 44.
39. Quoted in Shapiro, *Carlos Santana*, p. 86.

Chapter 3: The Big Time
40. Patrick MacDonald, e-mail message to author, March 2, 2006.
41. Leng, *Soul Sacrifice*, p. 57.
42. MacDonald, e-mail message to author.
43. Quoted in Heath, "The Epic Life of Carlos Santana."
44. Quoted in Heath, "The Epic Life of Carlos Santana."
45. Quoted in Heath, "The Epic Life of Carlos Santana."
46. Quoted in Shapiro, *Carlos Santana*, p. 98.
47. Quoted in Leng, *Soul Sacrifice*, p. 60.
48. Quoted in Shapiro, *Carlos Santana*, pp. 106–107.
49. Quoted in Heath, "The Epic Life of Carlos Santana."
50. Quoted in Shapiro, *Carlos Santana*, p. 134.

51. Quoted in Shapiro, *Carlos Santana*, p. 128.

52. Quoted in Shapiro, *Carlos Santana*, p. 150.

Chapter 4: *Love Devotion Surrender*

53. Quoted in Shapiro, *Carlos Santana*, p. 132.

54. Quoted in Tiscali, "Santana Biography." www.tiscali.co.uk/music/biography/santana_biography/2.

55. Quoted in Shapiro, *Carlos Santana*, p. 139.

56. Quoted in Santana, *Space Between the Stars*, p. 127.

57. Leng, *Soul Sacrifice*, p. 76.

58. Quoted in Heath, "The Epic Life of Carlos Santana."

59. Quoted in Heath, "The Epic Life of Carlos Santana."

60. Quoted in Heath, "The Epic Life of Carlos Santana."

61. Quoted in Leng, *Soul Sacrifice*, p. 79.

62. Quoted in Shapiro, *Carlos Santana*, p. 158.

Chapter 5: Holding Steady

63. Quoted in Shapiro, *Carlos Santana*, p. 165.

64. Santana, *Space Between the Stars*, p. 262.

65. Quoted in Shapiro, *Carlos Santana*, p. 166.

66. Quoted in Heath, "The Epic Life of Carlos Santana."

67. Quoted in Heath, "The Epic Life of Carlos Santana."

68. Quoted in Heilig, "Carlos Santana."

69. Quoted in Heilig, "Carlos Santana."

70. Quoted in Leng, *Soul Sacrifice*, p. 128.

71. Quoted in Shapiro, *Carlos Santana*, p. 169.

72. Quoted in Leng, *Soul Sacrifice*, p. 127.

73. Quoted in Leng, *Soul Sacrifice*, p. 129.

74. Quoted in Shapiro, *Carlos Santana*, pp. 179–80.

75. Quoted in Leng, *Soul Sacrifice*, p. 161.

76. Santana, *Space Between the Stars*, p. 290.

77. Quoted in Shapiro, *Carlos Santana*, p. 200.

78. Quoted in Heath, "The Epic Life of Carlos Santana."

79. Quoted in Heath, "The Epic Life of Carlos Santana."

80. Quoted in Heath, "The Epic Life of Carlos Santana."

81. Quoted in Heath, "The Epic Life of Carlos Santana."

82. Quoted in Heath, "The Epic Life of Carlos Santana."

83. Santana, *Space Between the Stars*, p. 316.

Chapter 6: Renewal

84. Quoted in Heath, "The Epic Life of Carlos Santana."

85. Leng, *Soul Sacrifice*, p. 179.

86. Quoted in Leng, *Soul Sacrifice*, p. 178.

87. Quoted in Thomson Gale, "Hispanic Heritages—Carlos Santana." www.gale.com/free_resources/chh/bio/santana_c.htm.

88. Quoted in Shapiro, *Carlos Santana*, pp. 4–5.

89. Quoted in Shapiro, *Carlos Santana*, p. 252.

90. Quoted in David Wild, "Supernatural," *Rolling Stone: Santana: Supernatural: Music Review.* www.rollingstone.com/artists/santana/albums/album/225609/rid/5941187/?rnd=1141752846270&has -player=true.

91. Quoted in Copley News Service, "Santana." www.loveandromance.com/features/get-features.asp?id=342&catid=17.

92. "Carlos Santana Speaks Out Against Bush," Newsday.com, March 21, 2006. www.newsday.com/entertainment/music/wire/sns-ap-peru-santana,0,2769084. story.

93. Quoted in Shapiro, *Carlos Santana*, p. 187.

94. Quoted in Heath, "The Epic Life of Carlos Santana."

95. Quoted in Heath, "The Epic Life of Carlos Santana."

96. Quoted in Heath, "The Epic Life of Carlos Santana."

97. Quoted in Heath, "The Epic Life of Carlos Santana."

Important Dates

1947
Carlos Augusto Alves Santana is born on July 20 in Autlán de Navarro, Jalisco, Mexico.

1955
Carlos, his mother, and siblings join their father in Tijuana.

1960
Carlos quits his first instrument, the violin, takes up the guitar, and gets his first real job, in a nightclub.

1962
Carlos becomes a citizen and forms his first band in America.

1966
Forms the Santana Blues Band.

1967
The Santana Blues Band makes its debut at the Fillmore Auditorium.

1968
Santana makes his recording debut on *The Live Adventures of Mike Bloomfield and Al Kooper.*

1969
The band skyrockets into national prominence after an appearance at the Woodstock Festival.

1971
The Santana Blues Band officially breaks up.

1973
Marries Deborah King.

1983
Salvador, the Santanas' first child, is born, followed by Stella in 1985 and Angelica in 1989.

1999
The album *Supernatural* is released to wide acclaim.

2001
Supernatural is nominated for eleven Grammy Awards and wins nine, including album of the year and song of the year.

2002
Santana continues his remarkable comeback with *Shaman*, another album of all-star duets.

2005
The guitarist releases *All That I Am*, which follows the winning duet format of previous albums.

2006
Santana's charitable organization, the Milagro Foundation, is honored by California Rural Legal Assistance, which fights for farmworkers and other needy Latinos.

For More Information

Books

Simon Leng, *Soul Sacrifice: The Santana Story.* London: FireFly, 2000. Less a biography than an analysis of Santana's music by a British music journalist. Contains a useful listing of the many musicians associated with Santana over the years.

Deborah Santana, *Space Between the Stars.* New York: Ballantine, 2005. An interesting memoir by the guitarist's wife and soul mate.

Marc Shapiro, *Carlos Santana: Back on Top.* New York: St. Martin's, 2000. A simply written celebrity biography.

Periodicals

Chris Heath, "The Epic Life of Carlos Santana," *Rolling Stone*, March 16, 2000. A far-ranging and incisive interview.

Steve Heilig, "Carlos Santana: An Interview with Steve Heilig," *Whole Earth*, Summer 2000. Another interview held in the wake of Santana's comeback with *Supernatural*.

David Wild, "Cosmic Carlos," *Rolling Stone*, August 19, 1999. A profile of the guitarist.

Web Sites

Hispanic Heritage—Biographies—Carlos Santana (www.gale.com/free_resources/chh/bio/santana_c.htm). This concise biography is part of the Gale Group's online service.

Santana (www.allmusicguide.com/cg/amg.dll?p=amg&token=&sql=11:33rx288c054). A useful site, part of the All Music Guide, that lists such things as former and current group members and bands that have been influenced by Santana over the years.

Santana Biography (www.tiscali.co.uk/music/biography/santana _biography.html). A good, short biography of the guitarist, part of a music-oriented Web site maintained by a British Internet service.

Santana Graduates from the Mission (www.sfmission.com/santana/earlyears.htm). This small but interesting site is maintained by an organization dedicated to promoting the Mission District of San Francisco, where Santana spent his teen years.

Santana.com—The Official Carlos Santana Web Site (www.santana.com). This authorized site has extensive historical and other information about Santana and his band over the years. There are also links to sites about his philanthropic foundation, his wife's book of memoirs, and more.

Santanamigos (http://perso.wanadoo.fr/santanamigos/menu.htm). This extensive Web site, maintained by fans, includes a detailed chronology of Santana's career and many reproductions of photos and posters.

Index

Picture Credits

About the Author

Adam Woog has written more than fifty books for adults, teens, and children. He has a special interest in music, and for Lucent Books his subjects have included Louis Armstrong, Duke Ellington, the Beatles, Elvis Presley, Ray Charles, Frank Sinatra, and histories of gospel, rock, and folk music. Woog lives with his wife and their daughter in Seattle, Washington.